OHIO PRESIDENTS SERIES

WILLIAM HENRY HARRISON

FATHER OF THE WEST

Sue Ann Painter

JARNDYCE & JARNDYCE PRESS
CINCINNATI BOOK PUBLISHERS

Dedicated to
W.W. Harrison, and his sisters, Madeline and Josephine

Author's Acknowledgments

My husband, Mark Painter, gave valuable advice and encouragement, for which I am grateful. Dr. Gary C. Ness, director emeritus of the Ohio Historical Society, and Dr. Larry Nelson, site manager of Fort Meigs, generously gave me access to the fort during their marvelous reconstruction, and provided illustrations and insights into William Henry Harrison's military reputation. Barrett J. Brunsman contributed to Chapter 2, and did the initial editing. Laura Chace and the staff of the Cincinnati Historical Society Library provided research assistance. George Dryer and Beverly Meyers of the Harrison-Symmes Museum and Paula Nossett of Grouseland Foundation provided illustrations from their superb collections.

The enthusiasm and generous assistance of these colleagues and allies made writing this book a joy. I also developed an appreciation for William Henry Harrison, whose leadership in shaping the Old Northwest has been undervalued. His life story and his legacy deserve to live on.

Editors: Barrett J. Brunsman and Mary E. Hull
Production: Cincinnati Book Publishing

Copyright: © 2004 Enslow Publishers, Inc.
All rights reserved. This edition published by Jarndyce & Jarndyce Press under license. No part of this book may be reproduced without permission of Enslow Publishers, www.enslow.com.

ISBN 0-9721916-1-5   paperback
ISBN 0-9721916-3-1   library edition
Library of Congress Control Number: 2004096630

Cover: *William Henry Harrison in 1814*, painting by Rembrandt Peale. Grouseland, Harrison Mansion Collection. Photo courtesy Grouseland Foundation.

To purchase additional books, visit www.cincybooks.com

Printed by John S. Swift Co., Inc., Cincinnati, OH

Contents

1	The Log Cabin Campaign	5
2	A Child of the Revolution	12
3	An Officer and a Gentleman	18
4	Aide to Anthony Wayne	23
5	Family Man and Governor	29
6	Battle of Tippecanoe	39
7	War of 1812	46
8	Civilian Life and Elected Office	56
9	Senator and U.S. Minister	67
10	Clod-Hopper Candidate	73
11	Log Cabin to the White House	80
12	Legacy	95

Chronology 100

Did You Know? 102

Chapter Notes 104

Further Reading and
 Internet Addresses 107

Places to Visit 108

Index 110

> ## SOURCE DOCUMENT
>
> # HARRISON!
> ### AND
> # REFORM!!
>
> **TO THE LOG CABIN BOYS.**
>
> *WILLIAM HENRY HARRISON, THE FARMER OF NORTH BEND.*
>
> You are, one and all, invited to attend a meeting of the friends of
>
> ## Harrison & Reform,
>
> At the OLD COURT ROOM, (Riley's Building,)
>
> ### On Saturday Evening next,
>
> **AT HALF PAST SEVEN,**
>
> To perfect the Arrangements necessary for the
>
> ## Springfield Convention,
>
> And also to attend to other important business.
>
> ☞ Citizens of Upper Alton, of Madison county, and all other LOG CABIN BOYS, are particularly invited to be present.
>
> Alton, May 19, 1840.
>
> J. A. NOBLE,
> Sec'ry Com. of Arrange.

A broadside from William Henry Harrison's 1840 campaign depicts him as a humble farmer at his plow.

1

The Log Cabin Campaign

They came from many miles and from many states. Men and women, aging war veterans and young businessmen, farmers and city slickers, took to the dusty country roads. Most traveled by horse-drawn buggy or wagon. Some arrived by boat from Lake Erie. In all, a crowd of more than twenty-five thousand people gathered for a political rally at Perrysburg, Ohio. It was June 11, 1840. At stake was the presidency of the United States.

The crowd was in a holiday mood. Campers spilled over the crumbling embankments of old Fort Meigs. The fort had been an important battle site in the War of 1812. General William Henry Harrison, the hero of Fort Meigs, was the main attraction at the rally. He was the first westerner, first Ohioan, and first Whig party candidate for president. The people loved him, and they showed it.

The crowd feasted on free barbeque and hard cider. People paraded and danced, and they chanted the campaign slogan, "Old Tippecanoe and Tyler Too." Harrison was called "Tippecanoe" after an Indiana battleground where he had once won a victory over the Indians. John Tyler was his vice-presidential running mate. Rally-goers applauded the lengthy speeches. They listened to glee clubs and joyously sang along. Everyone forgot the hard times of the economic depression. Since 1837, the nation had suffered from financial hard times. Money was scarce and people were out of work. The rally provided needed entertainment. Best of all, it was free.

Campaign workers gave away souvenir songbooks, ribbons, miniature jugs, and plates. The souvenirs bore symbols of everyday things that common people could relate to. Most westerners were farmers and their first house was a log cabin. So the souvenir jugs were in the shape of a log cabin. Some were filled with hard cider, an alcoholic beverage. Other giveaways had pictures of cabins, farm fields, or a man plowing. Harrison's campaign became known as the "Log Cabin campaign."

At the Fort Meigs rally, sixty-seven-year old William Henry Harrison spoke for an hour. He recalled the events that happened in that place. He spoke in the language of a patriot—one who loves his country. He remembered the brave Americans who had held off two long British attacks upon the fort.

Only adult white males could vote then. But women loved Harrison, too. He had helped protect them or their pioneer mothers from the Indians, and women were part of the diverse crowd that gathered to hear Harrison speak. Some Native Americans participated happily in the

THE LOG CABIN CAMPAIGN

William Henry Harrison used his War of 1812 reputation to help win the presidency in 1840. In this campaign broadside, Harrison extends a hand to a disabled veteran and directs him to a barrel of hard cider.

rally. They had suffered terrible injustices under former President Andrew Jackson's Indian Removal Act of 1832. They expected better if Harrison won the White House. He was running against Jackson's hand picked successor, President Martin Van Buren.

Even a few free African Americans came to Log Cabin events. The general's political opponents made sure this was known in the South. They warned that because African Americans were allowed at his rallies, Harrison favored freedom for slaves. They said inviting the Native American dancers was also insulting. It proved he still trusted the enemy. But these Ohio Native Americans had helped Harrison defeat the British in the War of 1812. He called them friends.

General Harrison was not a revolutionary or a reformer. But he was the son of a revolutionary. And he had spent his adult life in the democratic society of the Northwest Territory. He had shared the hardships of the pioneers and the frontier militia. He was born to wealth, but he had worked hard all his life. He was a generous and compassionate man. And he understood the concerns of small farmers and laborers. He welcomed their support.

Unlike Harrison's 1840 campaign, early American elections had been quiet and proper. Our first presidents, George Washington and John Adams, did not want to be caught campaigning, or "electioneering," as it was called then. They rarely spoke to gatherings of common people. They did not make campaign promises. They did not tell people government would help them. Candidates debated issues in the newspapers. Sometimes, they wrote cruel and vicious letters about their opponents. Campaigns were often nasty, but they were seldom filled with emotion, high spirits, laughter, or song.

By the 1820s and 1830s, politics had become something of a popular sport. Common men—those who did not own property or a business—even began to run for office. General Andrew Jackson was the first presidential candidate to brag about his humble origins. He described himself as a self-made man. He claimed to be "the people's president." The strategy worked. Jackson was elected twice, in 1828 and 1832.

The first presidents, George Washington and John Adams, disapproved of political parties. But parties grew in importance. By the 1830s, politicians realized that new

THE LOG CABIN CAMPAIGN

Harrison is shown as a patriot, farmer, soldier, and statesman in this poster from his campaign for the presidency. The Whig campaign of 1840 brought supporters together at large festive rallies that were part entertainment, part politics.

middle-class voters were becoming more numerous and powerful than rich ones. Harrison was the candidate of a new party created in the 1830s called the Whig Party. Party members were united by their dislike of "King Andrew," as they called President Jackson. They also disliked Jackson's chosen successor, Martin Van Buren, who had defeated Harrison in the presidential election of 1836. The two men opposed one another again in 1840.

Harrison's political advisors had seen General Jackson's popularity with the common man. They thought General Harrison had some of the same popular appeal.

Ninth president of the United States William Henry Harrison.

They promoted their candidate as the humble "Farmer of North Bend." In fact, Harrison's father was a Virginia plantation owner and his wife, Anna Symmes, was the daughter of a large property owner in Ohio. Her father's old log cabin where the couple lived had been converted into a large, wood-paneled house.

An Eastern newspaper, the *Baltimore Sun,* gave the Whigs their winning campaign theme. Its editor dismissed

Harrison as an aging country bumpkin. He wrote that if given a small pension, Harrison would retire to his log cabin. He would happily live out his days with a jug of hard cider. The writer meant to insult the candidate. But Harrison's backers liked the description. It was a perfect contrast to his Democratic opponent "Prince Matty" Van Buren, who put on aristocratic airs. The log cabin and jug of hard cider became symbols for the Harrison campaign.

Today, the Log Cabin campaign is recognized as the first modern political campaign. It changed American politics forever, and it became a model for our times.

The crowd at Fort Meigs sang far into the night. They rolled a giant parade ball, and chanted silly, memorable songs like "Keep the Ball a' Rollin." And everyone had a jolly good time.[1]

2

A CHILD OF THE REVOLUTION

William Henry Harrison was born on February 9, 1773, in the bedroom of his mother. Her name was Elizabeth Bassett Harrison, and her room was on the second floor of a brick home in Charles City County, Virginia. His father, Benjamin Harrison, was a wealthy landowner.

Their home was the main building on a large farm named Berkeley. Such a building is called a manor house. Today, Berkeley is still a farm. Around 450 of its 1,000 acres are used to grow crops. But when William Henry was a child, the farm covered tens of thousands of acres. It was one of the biggest plantations in America.

William Henry's great-great-great grandfather, Benjamin I, was the first Harrison to live in America. He traveled from England to the colony of Virginia around 1632.

A CHILD OF THE REVOLUTION

Benjamin Harrison I didn't have a lot of money when he arrived in Virginia. But he could read and write, so he got a job as the clerk of the Council of Landowners. The Council advised a governor from England on what kinds of laws Virginia should have. Benjamin made friends with these rich landowners, and he began buying land himself. Eventually, he owned about seven hundred acres. Each Harrison generation bought more land. By the time William Henry's father, Benjamin V, inherited the property, the Harrisons were among the largest landowners in Virginia.

William Henry's dad planted crops such as tobacco. Tobacco was known as a cash crop because farmers sold it instead of eating it or feeding it to their animals.

William Henry Harrison was born at Berkeley Plantation in Charles City, Virginia, where his father grew thousands of acres of tobacco.

Virginia planters sold tobacco to people in England and other European countries.

William Henry's dad also built ships in a yard next to the James River. The river runs alongside Berkeley Plantation for three miles and leads to the Atlantic Ocean. He used the ships to transport the tobacco he grew. And other farmers paid him to ship their tobacco across the ocean so it could be sold in Europe. The ships would bring back manufactured goods such as clothing. Benjamin Harrison V sold the imported goods to his neighbors in Virginia.

Because he was a smart businessman, Benjamin Harrison V made a lot of money. So William Henry Harrison grew up in one of the wealthiest families in America. He had four sisters and two brothers. Their names were Elizabeth, Anne, Benjamin VI, Lucy, Carter, and Sarah. William Henry was the youngest.

The Harrisons weren't the only people who lived at Berkeley Plantation. Much of the work was done by slaves from Africa and indentured servants from Europe.

There were no schools nearby when William Henry Harrison was a boy. So a teacher came to the manor house and taught him there. He learned about history, math, and writing. He also studied two foreign languages, Latin and Greek.

William Henry liked to read, especially books about history. And every Sunday, he read the Bible. His family worshiped God at the nearby Westover Episcopal Church. Built in 1730, the small brick building is one of the oldest churches in America.

Because William Henry's father was active in politics and liked to entertain people, many presidents dined at

A CHILD OF THE REVOLUTION

their manor house. Benjamin Harrison V served as governor of Virginia three times, including during the Revolutionary War. As a result, William Henry got to meet some famous men when he was a boy. George Washington, the first president of the United States, even bounced William Henry on his knee when he was a baby. Martha Washington's sister was William Henry's aunt.[1]

William Henry's father was one of the signers of the Declaration of Independence. In that document, Americans declared that they wanted to be independent of Great Britain so they could form their own country. But the ruler of Britain, King George III of England, sent an army to America to force the colonists to stay loyal to him. Americans revolted, and a deadly war began. During the Revolutionary War, which lasted from 1775 to 1781, the Harrison shipyard on the James River at Berkeley built wooden gunships for the American Navy.

General Benedict Arnold, who had switched sides from the American Army and joined the British, arrived at Berkeley on January 4, 1781. The traitor Arnold had two thousand British troops with him. They hoped to capture William Henry's father. But Benjamin Harrison was too smart to get caught. He sent William Henry, then eight years old, and the rest of the family to stay at a nearby plantation owned by some relatives. Then he went to Philadelphia, Pennsylvania, to get help from the American Army. Furious that Harrison had eluded him, General Arnold had his Redcoats burn the family's portraits and furniture on the lawn outside the Berkeley manor house. The British also shot some of the farm animals and stole forty slaves.

This was not the first time Berkeley Plantation had

SOURCE DOCUMENT

William Henry Harrison's father was one of the signers of the Declaration of Independence, the document that asserted America's independence from Great Britain.

been attacked. In 1622 American Indians killed dozens of the European settlers at the plantation. Later, a secret tunnel was built under the ground between the Berkeley manor house and a smaller house nearby. Built by William Henry's grandparents around 1726, this tunnel gave family members a chance to escape if the Indians ever attacked again. But they never did.

When William Henry Harrison was growing up, he liked to play doctor. Sometimes he put bandages on members of his family, the servants, and even his pets. He pretended they were hurt so he could take care of them.[2]

William Henry's father thought his son might someday want to have a job as a real doctor. So when the boy was fourteen, his dad sent him to Hampden-Sydney College in Virginia. It had a reputation for training people who would become doctors. While in college, William Henry studied more Greek, Latin, math, and history. He especially liked reading history books about heroic soldiers from Rome and Greece.

After college, William Henry served as an apprentice to Dr. Andrew Leiper, a surgeon in Richmond, Virginia. In 1790, William Henry traveled to Philadelphia to study medicine at the University of Pennsylvania. This was considered the best medical school in the country. It was run by Dr. Benjamin Rush, who had signed the Declaration of Independence in 1776 along with Benjamin Harrison.

While William Henry was at the University of Pennsylvania, his father died. He was only halfway through with the thirty-two-week medical school, and his dad had wanted him to become a doctor. But instead of finishing school, William decided it might be more fun to become a soldier like the ones he had read about.

An Officer and a Gentleman

At the age of eighteen, William Henry Harrison went to visit the most famous soldier in America. This man, who happened to be an old friend of his dad, was George Washington. He had served as the general in charge of the American Army during the Revolutionary War. In 1789, Washington had been elected the first president of the United States. Philadelphia was the nation's capital at the time, so President Washington was in the same city where Harrison was going to medical school. As commander in chief of the American military, Washington could give Harrison a job.

The president signed papers making Harrison an ensign, which was the lowest rank for an officer. His first assignment was to find other young men who would join the military. Then Ensign William Henry Harrison was to lead the men to the American frontier. Back in

President George Washington, made William Henry Harrison an ensign with the American Army in 1791.

1791, that meant traveling to Fort Washington along the Ohio River to what is now Cincinnati, Ohio.

This was considered a dangerous assignment because the Indians who lived near Cincinnati weren't always friendly. Sometimes they attacked the white settlers who moved to the Ohio Country. The Indians were mad that the settlers hunted for the same animals they depended on for food. And the Indians didn't like it when the settlers chopped down trees to farm the land. The Indians figured they had been there first, so the land belonged to them. The job of Ensign Harrison and his men was to protect the settlers from hostile Indians. That meant the soldiers had to be prepared to risk their lives by fighting the Native Americans.

Harrison was going to a place where there were more opportunities than in the older southern and eastern states. Land was plentiful and cheap on the frontier. A poor man could make a good living here. A man like Harrison with a little money to invest might become rich. But there were no fine brick houses or paved streets. There were no cities like Philadelphia or Boston. The Ohio Country was beautiful and full of promise. But it was also a dangerous wilderness. Angry Indians were killing and

Ensign Harrison was sent to the frontier to protect settlers from unfriendly Indians.

terrorizing the settlers. They hoped to drive them back across the Ohio River.

President Washington was in a difficult situation. He did not want war with Native Americans, and he had only a small army to command. But he had to protect American citizens. He sent General Josiah Harmar, a Revolutionary War veteran, to Fort Washington.

Most of the soldiers were untrained militia. All healthy adult men could be called to military duty for six months. The federal government was supposed to pay the militia three dollars a month. But many times, the soldiers were not paid, so they deserted. The militia was always short of food and ammunition. The system did not work well.

Harmar's soldiers burned the villages and cornfields of the Miami and Shawnee Indian tribes. Led by Miami Chief Little Turtle, the Indians fought back. They defeated the American Army. The next commander of the U.S. Army was the governor of the Northwest Territory, Arthur St. Clair. He was another veteran of the Revolution. In November 1791, he marched north with fourteen hundred men. Little Turtle struck again. More than half the U.S. Army was killed. It was the worst military defeat in the nation's history.

Women, who were called camp followers, and their children traveled with the U.S. Army. They were the cooks, nurses, and wives of the soldiers. Of the two hundred women and children, only three survived the assault led by Little Turtle.

President Washington removed both generals. He had convinced Congress of the need for a professional army, called the Legion of the United States. He selected General Anthony Wayne, a younger Revolutionary War veteran, as commander. But it would be another year before Wayne's forces traveled to Ohio.

Ensign Harrison and his men arrived in Cincinnati on November 21, 1791, just as St. Clair's surviving soldiers were straggling into Fort Washington. Their stories were chilling. Eighteen-year-old William Henry Harrison got a bloody introduction to the frontier.

Colonel James Wilkerson was the senior officer at the fort. At first, Wilkerson and his officers resented Ensign Harrison. Harrison was an officer because of his family connections to the president. He had no military training. His men were inexperienced street toughs. The veterans thought Harrison would quit before long.

Cincinnati was a small, dirty town. The barracks was a rough place. There was no recreation except gambling, drinking, and dueling. Soldiers thought that an honorable man was obliged to duel—or engage in combat in the presence of witnesses—when insulted or challenged. Harrison disagreed. He refused to fight in duels.

One officer from Virginia knew the Harrison family. He gave the boy a friendly warning, telling him that if he stayed in the service he would probably become a drunk and a gambler like the rest.[1] But Harrison surprised them all. He showed strength of character and good judgment. He set a good example by his personal habits. He did not

> **SOURCE DOCUMENT**

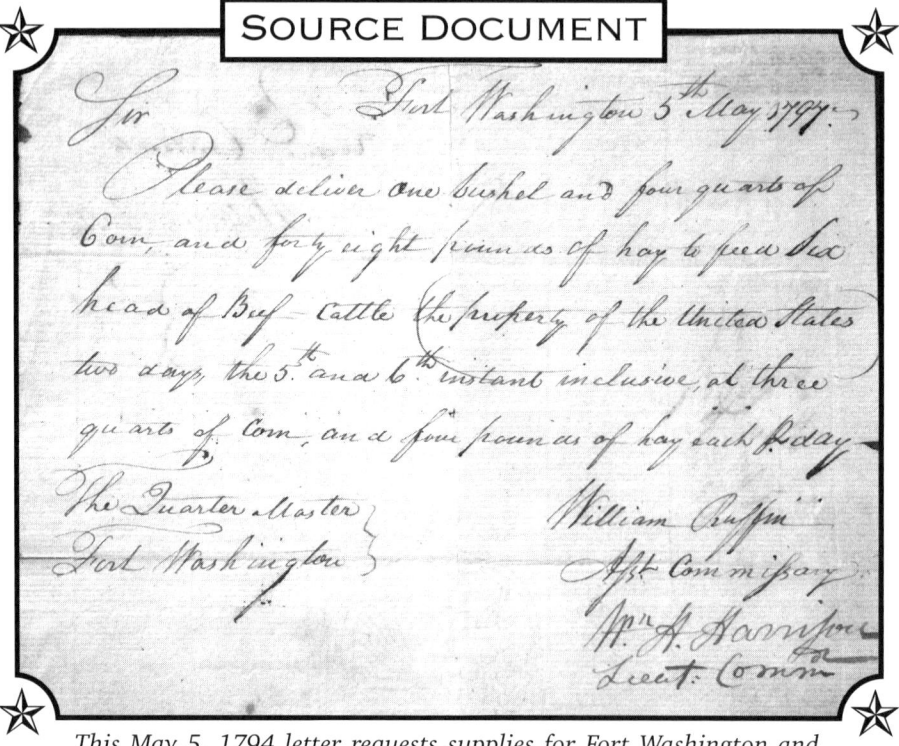

This May 5, 1794 letter requests supplies for Fort Washington and was signed by William Henry Harrison.

drink hard liquor. He was kind and loyal to his men. In turn, they were loyal to him. He read every book he could find on the military. Wilkerson sent Harrison out on some dangerous missions. Ensign Harrison passed these tests, returning safely. He soon won the respect of his fellow officers. They realized he was young, but not immature.

Colonel Wilkerson was impressed by the ensign's performance and his good manners. He trusted Harrison to escort his wife and three young sons back to school in Philadelphia. On that trip in the summer of 1792, Harrison got a lucky break—one that helped advance his career.

4

Aide to Anthony Wayne

Ensign Harrison accompanied Colonel Wilkerson's family by riverboat to Pittsburgh, Pennsylvania. From there, they traveled by horse-drawn coach to Philadelphia. In Pittsburgh, the party met General Anthony Wayne, who was drilling new soldiers. Wayne was impressed with young Harrison. The two met again when Wayne arrived in Fort Washington in April 1793. Wayne promoted Harrison to lieutenant and made him one of three aides-de-camp. This meant he became one of Wayne's three closest military assistants. It gave Harrison a pay raise to around six hundred dollars a year.

Harrison was fascinated by the ancient Indian earth mounds near the town, and he took the general to see them. The tallest mound was more than fifty feet high. Wayne decided the field where that mound stood would be the campsite for the Legion of the United States.

Harrison's first lessons in military science had come from books. But his real education came from working as aide to General Wayne. For the rest of his life, Harrison praised Wayne as his teacher. The most important lesson he learned was to always be prepared.

The United States did not want war with the Indians. Throughout the spring and summer of 1793, there were peace talks. The British Canadians offered to help bring the sides together. Later, the Americans suspected they had encouraged the Indians to keep on fighting. The talks went on for months and nothing changed. The Indians insisted there would be war unless all white settlers returned East. President Washington found this unacceptable. It was, in fact, impossible for him to hold back the land-hungry settlers.

There were no Indian villages in the Cincinnati region when the white settlers arrived. The architects of the mysterious earth mounds Harrison showed Wayne had left the area around eight hundred years earlier. But a number of powerful tribes—the Delaware, Iroquois, Miami, Mingo, Seneca, and Shawnee—were in the territory for part of each year. These tribes used the forests as their hunting grounds. They kept houses and raised crops in villages in Northern Ohio. The Indians did not keep farm animals, but they planted, harvested, and stored corn for the winter. The women were capable farmers. They grew corn and squash in fields that covered many acres. It was the men's job to hunt, and to defend the women and children.

European Americans and Native Americans were very different. They differed in race, religion, and lifestyle. Native Americans lived in communities, like one large family. Within the tribe, work and wealth were shared.

General Anthony Wayne, at right, made Harrison one of his assistants and educated him in the ways of the military.

Land could not belong to a single person. Most European Americans found these practices backward, They believed the American Indians thought like children and they called them "savages." European Americans and Native Americans could not agree. Each side thought the other was wrong. With such large differences, conflict was hard to avoid.

The Indians controlled all of the Ohio Country except for a strip along the river at Cincinnati. Wayne's Legion left from there in 1793 to find and battle the Indians. The Indians lived along the Maumee River, not far from Lake Erie. In between were hundreds of miles of wilderness. The land was covered with trees and underbrush.

Hostile Indians lurked in the forests. They were experts at stealing horses and cattle from the supply lines. Wayne built forts along the military road to store supplies. Halfway to Lake Erie, Wayne received orders to halt. Winter was near, and President Washington did not wish to risk another great loss. The Legion camped at Fort Greenville, where Lieutenant Harrison and his fellow officers drilled and rehearsed the men.

Indian scouts were watching. They reported that General Wayne was a cautious and capable commander. Miami Chief Little Turtle, who had destroyed the armies of General Hamar and General St. Clair, advised the tribes

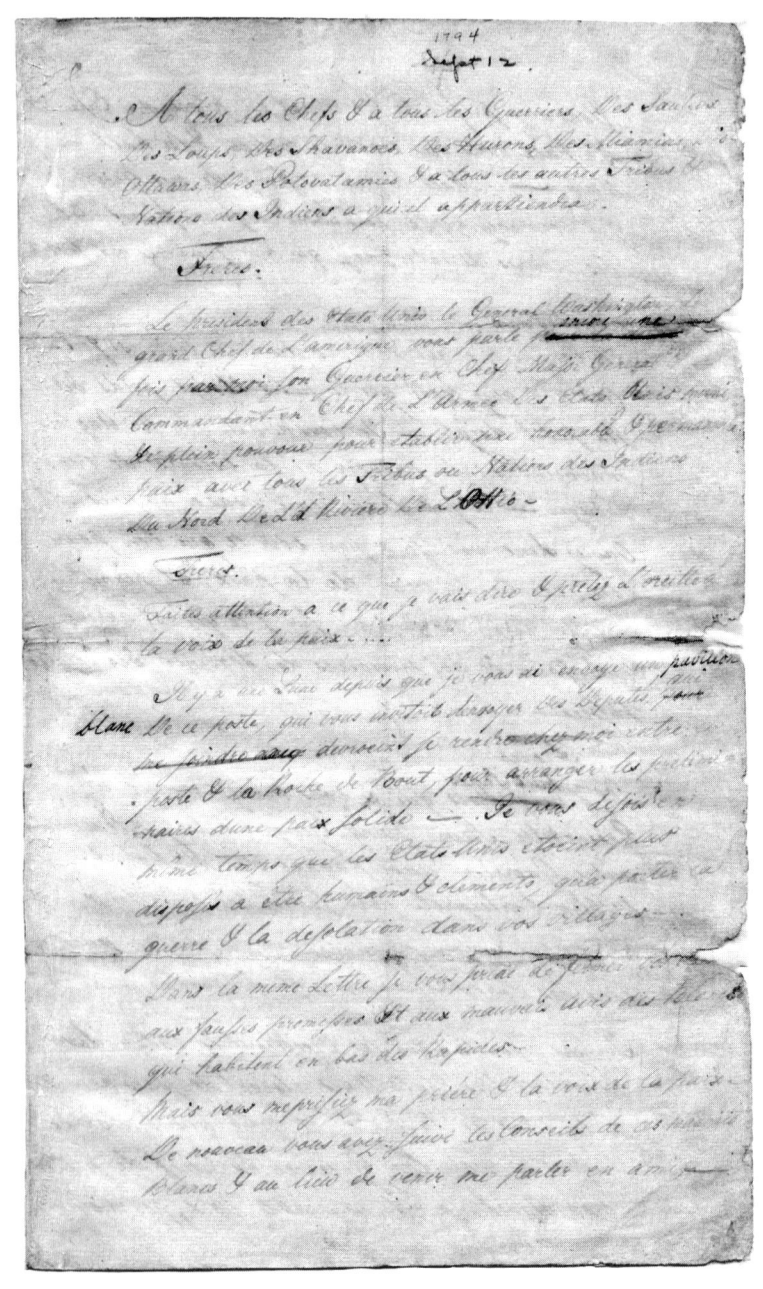

General Anthony Wayne wrote this letter to the northern Indian tribes defeated at the Battle of Fallen Timbers, calling for peace.

to seek peace. "You have been successful twice," he said, "but you cannot always expect to succeed; you have to fight an officer now who never sleeps."[1] The younger warriors scoffed. Little Turtle was removed from command. The war was on.

The Legion of the United States met the Indians on August 20, 1794, in an area near the Maumee River. Later, the clash became known as the Battle of Fallen Timbers. A great windstorm had uprooted a number of large trees. The warriors hid among the logs, where they could fire their guns from cover. Shawnee Chief Blue Jacket led the Native American warriors. The Americans fought bravely and well. There were losses on both sides. Finally, the Indians fled. Lieutenant Harrison's first real battle was a victory.

Wayne had three aides. Two had stayed behind the line to protect him. Harrison, the third aide, was in the heart of the battle. He was in constant danger as he galloped across the fields, delivering commands from Wayne to the officers. Harrison credited his gallant horse, "Fearnaught," for carrying him swiftly about the battlefield. Afterward, General Wayne praised Harrison in his reports.

Other soldiers were impressed with Harrison's coolness under fire. Lieutenant Thomas Underwood kept a journal of his war service. He wrote about Harrison at Fallen Timbers, saying, "It is my candid opinion if he continues a military man he will be a second Washington."[2] No American officer was held in higher regard than George Washington. There could be no stronger praise.

Fallen Timbers was a major defeat for the Native Americans in Ohio. They were eager to make peace. In the spring and summer, both sides met frequently. The Treaty of Greenville was signed August 3, 1795, by ninety-two Indian leaders (including Miami Chief Little Turtle) and twenty-seven U.S. representatives. Harrison wrote portions of the document. He took it to the printer in Lexington, and he was one of the signers.

In the treaty, the Indians gave the lower two-thirds of Ohio to the United States government, and they agreed to keep the peace.

There were a few holdouts. Most notable for his absence was the young Shawnee warrior, Tecumseh. He had refused to deal with the white men and give up the Shawnee claim to the Northwest Territory. While the Americans rejoiced over the signing of the treaty, Tecumseh's unhappiness went unnoticed.

Settlers poured into the Ohio Valley as soon as the treaty was announced. In ten years, the Ohio Territory grew by 483 percent. The Battle of Fallen Timbers and the Treaty of Greenville opened the area to settlement.

Harrison's peacetime assignment was to see that the treaty was observed. In this work, he made friends with several chiefs. Some would later become his allies in the War of 1812. Harrison also became lifelong friends with a number of his young fellow soldiers. Several became important names in American history. Meriwether Lewis would eventually team with another Fallen Timbers veteran, William Clark, to explore the far West. Captain Montgomery Zebulon Pike was another explorer who would one day leave his name on Pike's Peak in Colorado.

5

Family Man and Governor

In April 1795, General Wayne sent Harrison on business to Lexington, Kentucky. The young officer was invited to the Lexington estate of Major Peyton Short and his wife, Maria. There, Harrison met Maria's sister, Anna Symmes. He described her as a "remarkably beautiful girl."[1] Anna was traveling to the family home in North Bend, fifteen miles west of Cincinnati. Her father, John Cleves Symmes, was a judge of the Northwest Territory and a large landowner.

According to family tradition, it was love at first sight.[2] Harrison returned to Fort Greenville, where he signed the treaty in August. But he did not forget the lovely brown-eyed girl. Back at Fort Washington in late summer, he found reason to escort some packhorses to North Bend. He spent time visiting Anna at her home. She shared his spirit of adventure and love for the Ohio

Country. She was an excellent horsewoman who fearlessly galloped across the wooded hills of North Bend. The handsome young man made her "the offer of his hand" in marriage.[3]

Anna's father was not pleased with Harrison as a prospective son-in-law. Judge Symmes wrote his friend Robert Morris that the young man had "understanding, prudence, education, & resource in conversation . . . Abilities he has, what his application may be I have yet to discover . . . He has no profession but that of arms."[4] Symmes had given his daughter a boarding school education, rare for the time. He thought she could do better.

Apparently the women of the Symmes family approved of Harrison. They arranged a wedding at the Symmes home on November 25, 1795, the day before Thanksgiving. Maria and Peyton Short traveled from Lexington. The stylish Susan Livingston Symmes, Anna's stepmother and friend, was the hostess. There was no church or minister in the country. So the township justice of the peace, Dr. Stephen Wood, was asked to perform the ceremony. Judge Symmes may not have realized the family gathering was to include a wedding. He jumped on his horse and rode away. Anna, at age twenty-two, had a mind of her own. The wedding went on without him.

The newlyweds moved into two rooms of a blockhouse at Fort Washington. The officers' quarters were at the eastern end of the blockhouse, next to a garden. The little home was large enough for guests. Mrs. Symmes stayed with the Harrisons when the judge was out in the territory. Little Turtle, the great Miami chief, stopped to spend a few days with the Harrisons. He was returning to his home in northern Ohio from Philadelphia, where he

Though this picture is from her later years, Anna Symmes was just twenty-two when she became William Henry Harrison's wife.

had visited President John Adams. The chief enjoyed talking about the important people he met in the U.S. capital.[5] (The capital was not moved to Washington, D.C., until 1800.)

General Wayne had made Harrison a captain and commandant of the fort in 1797. But he found the pay too low, especially now that he was a family man. In September 1797, their first daughter had been born at the fort. Named Elizabeth Bassett Harrison for William Henry's mother, the girl was called Betsy. Harrison resigned from his post to become a registrar in the land office. A son was born in 1798, and they named him John Cleves Symmes Harrison for Anna's father. They called him Symmes.

Cincinnati was a small town with big opportunities. William Henry Harrison participated in community life. He gave money to build the first Presbyterian Church. He made new friends. And he kept in touch with old friends in the East. His friends came through for him with an important job. On June 28, 1798, President John Adams appointed Harrison secretary of the Northwest Territory. The secretary was second only to the governor, Arthur St. Clair, in running the Northwest Territory.

St. Clair and Harrison disagreed on politics. St. Clair

was a Federalist, the political party of Alexander Hamilton. Governor St. Clair was reluctant to introduce self-government in the territory because he wanted only men of education and property to have a voice. He did not think most of the pioneer settlers were educated enough to vote. Although Harrison was appointed by the Federalist administration, he liked many of the ideas of his fellow Virginian, Thomas Jefferson, and the Democratic-Republican Party. Like Jefferson, Harrison believed that Americans had fought the Revolution so that ordinary working people could govern themselves.

Self-government in the territory slowly moved forward. Congress ordered an election for 1799. White males owning fifty acres or more were allowed to vote. Those owning two hundred acres or more could run for office. A twenty-two-member assembly was elected. The assembly then voted on a representative to the United States Congress. Two candidates were nominated: William Henry Harrison and Arthur St. Clair Jr. With the help of the transplanted Virginia Jeffersonians in Chillicothe, Ohio, the twenty-six-year-old Harrison won the close election in September 1799. He was considered a Democratic-Republican by this time, but he stayed friendly with leaders of both parties.[6]

There must have been a lot of excitement in the Harrison household after the election. Because Congress was still in session in Philadelphia, Harrison and his wife Anna, along with Betsy, now age three, and Symmes, age one, left immediately. On December 6, Harrison took his seat in Independence Hall. His father, Benjamin, had sat in the Continental Congress in the same room. And here was William Henry, making history as the first delegate

FAMILY MAN AND GOVERNOR

from the Northwest Territory. Judge Symmes' daughter had chosen a rising star.

Because Ohio was not yet a state, Harrison could not vote. But he could propose legislation. He wrote and championed an important bill known as the Harrison Land Law of 1800. It enabled individuals to purchase small parcels of land from the government, and it allowed people to buy land on credit. The price was two dollars an acre. It made the American Dream of owning one's own home and farm possible for many people.

Nothing like this opportunity was available anywhere else in the world. The people of the territory were pleased with Representative Harrison. The Land Act was one of Harrison's major accomplishments, and it shaped the settlement of the West.

Harrison sponsored another bill in 1800, and it had an immediate impact upon his career. This proposal divided the Northwest Territory into two parts. Ohio, which had grown swiftly in population, was preparing to become a state in 1803. So it was separated from the rest of the Northwest Territory. The remaining section was named the Indiana Territory. Congress passed Harrison's bill. Vincennes, an old French town on the Wabash River, was made the capital of the new Indiana Territory.

Representative Harrison had impressed government leaders in Washington. Before Congress adjourned, President Adams invited him to become governor of the Indiana Territory. Harrison was younger than most governors in the colonial and federal periods, but he had useful experience for this very important job. He would command the militia and negotiate with the Indians. He and the three new judges for the territory would adopt laws and set up

SOURCE DOCUMENT

AMENDMENTS

OF THE

SENATE,

TO THE BILL,

INTITULED,

" AN ACT TO AMEND THE ACT INTITULED " AN ACT PROVIDING FOR THE SALE OF THE LANDS OF THE

UNITED STATES,

NORTH-WEST OF THE OHIO,

AND ABOVE THE MOUTH OF

KENTUCKY RIVER.

23d. April, 1800.

Referred to Mr. Harrifon, Mr. Brace, Mr. Gordon, Mr. Lyman, Mr. Davis, Mr. Grove, and Mr. Gallatin.

Shortly after being elected as the Northwest Territory's delegate to Congress, Harrison helped sponsor the Land Law of 1800, which expanded the opportunity of Americans to buy land from the government.

a system of government. Harrison had already done these things on the Ohio frontier.

The Harrisons must have been a little nervous about leaving friends and family. They were going to a place that was almost like a foreign country. The people of Vincennes were mostly French traders. Many of the men had married Indian women. Only a few spoke English. Vincennes was in the wilderness, nearly three hundred miles west of Cincinnati, Ohio. There were no roads. William Henry rode cross-country on horseback. Anna followed several months later. Already she was mother to three children under the age of four. Another daughter, Lucy, had been born in 1800.

Anna's stepmother, Susan Symmes, helped move the family and its belongings to Vincennes. They went by flatboat down the Ohio River to Louisville, Kentucky. Governor Harrison met his family there. The passengers and furniture were transferred to smaller keel boats, which could be poled up the Wabash River. The journey took one month. Mrs. Symmes wrote friends back East, describing the exceptional beauty of the spring landscape.

The residents of Vincennes greeted the Harrisons warmly. The family lived with Francis Vigo, the leading citizen, for more than a year. Then they built a grand home of their own on four hundred acres. The architectural style was much like Harrison's childhood home in Virginia. It even had a secret underground tunnel to the Wabash River in case of enemy attacks. The estate was named "Grouseland," because of all the grouse, or game birds, in the fields. Harrison enjoyed hunting grouse.

Governor and Mrs. Harrison entertained many visitors at Grouseland. No stranger went away without a meal at their table. The governor's job paid two thousand dollars a year, and Harrison spent a lot of his salary on his guests.

In 1803, the United States purchased the Louisiana Territory from the French. President Thomas Jefferson made Upper Louisiana part of the Indiana Territory. He made Harrison governor of it all. In October 1804, Governor Harrison traveled by horseback to St. Louis in the Louisiana Purchase to meet the new U.S. citizens.

The residents of St. Louis were French, as in Vincennes. But St. Louis was a larger and more sophisticated city. Harrison was entertained at grand dinner parties. Meriwether Lewis and William Clark were also in St. Louis at this time, preparing for their western expedition. President Jefferson was sending them out to chart the route from the Mississippi River, up the Missouri River, to the Pacific Ocean. Upon their return, they would send Governor Harrison a map from the two-year trek across the Rocky Mountains. It was a very exciting time in American history.

Indiana was slower to grow than Ohio had been. Some early settlers argued that wealthy Virginians would migrate to the new territories if slavery were permitted there. The French who occupied Vincennes and St. Louis kept slaves. Slavery had been prohibited in the Northwest Territory by the Northwest Ordinance. The Ordinance was the legal code adopted by Congress, which governed the Northwest Territory before statehood. Some settlers migrated to the territory because they did not wish to live in a slave state. The Indiana legislature discussed allowing settlers to bring in slaves for a ten-year period. A Quaker antislavery group protested and stopped that from happening. Indentured servitude was permitted,

As governor of the Indiana Territory, Harrison had this home, called "Grouseland," built for his family.

however, if the servant signed a contract. In some cases, the results were much like slavery.

Historians disagree on the extent of Governor Harrison's support for these measures. Evidence indicates that he supported attempts to introduce involuntary servitude, in one form or other, on a temporary basis. In later years, Harrison readily admitted to bringing slaves into Ohio. But he boasted that by doing so, he set them free.[7] In Ohio, the former slaves could expect to work six to eight years without pay in return for room, board, and liberty.

One of Harrison's primary assignments from Presidents Adams and Jefferson was to buy land from the Native Americans. Jefferson wrote Harrison urging him to tell the Indians they must learn to live and farm like white people. The president said he would:

> be glad to see the good and influential individuals among them run into debt, because we observe that when these debts get beyond what the Indians can pay, they become willing to lop them off by a cession of lands."[8]

Some historians have faulted Harrison for taking unfair advantage of Native Americans with his big land grabs. But the blame must be shared with the presidents Harrison served under. The price the Indians were paid per acre was ridiculously low. Harrison asked for increased funds, but they were not granted. The amount of wilderness land was vast, and the Indian population was small. If the government did not buy their land, white settlers would steal it. As many tribes realized, Native Americans had little choice.

The situation between European Americans and Native Americans in the Indiana Territory became tense after 1807. That year, the British Navy attacked the American ship the *Chesapeake*. There was strong talk of war. The British Canadians wanted the Indians on their side if the Americans tried to invade Canada. So they increased their gifts of food and firearms to the tribes.

In 1809, Harrison negotiated the Treaty of Fort Wayne, which ceded 3 million acres of Indian lands to the U.S. government. The deal was struck with the help of his friend Little Turtle. The Miami and several other tribes signed over the land in Indiana for pennies an acre, but not everyone was happy with the bargain.

Battle of Tippecanoe

Two men came to represent the conflict between red and white men on the western frontier: William Henry Harrison and Tecumseh. Tecumseh and his brother, who was called the Prophet, were Shawnees. At first, the Prophet was the more important. He was a religious leader who attracted converts from different tribes throughout the Northwest. He led them to a settlement in northern Indiana called Prophetstown. His followers were instructed to return to a Native American lifestyle. They were to dress and work in traditional Indian ways. They were not to drink the white man's liquor.

Tecumseh was a brilliant military leader, and he built a following. He wanted the various tribes to stop warring against one another. He explained that Native Americans should work together to remove the white intruders. He

Tecumseh, the leader of the Shawnees, tried to join the Indian tribes together into a confederation to oppose the advance of the white settlers.

was outraged by the Treaty of Fort Wayne. The Shawnee had not signed the agreement. Tecumseh took the dispute directly to Harrison. The chief traveled to Grouseland in 1810. He was accompanied by four hundred armed and painted warriors. They came down the Wabash River in eighty canoes. It was an awesome sight.

Tecumseh was a dramatic and powerful speaker. He opened the council by reciting a long list of grievances against the United States government. He told the history of the Indians, a "once happy race, but now made miserable by the white people, who are never contented."[1] He observed the Native Americans had been pushed from the East coast, and that the whites were now trying to "push us into the lakes."[2] He agreed that Indians could sell land, but he thought that all the tribes must join in the agreement to make it legal.

Governor Harrison argued that his treaties were based upon common consent. More than one-third of the territory's Indian population had witnessed the Fort Wayne document. Even more people showed up to collect the annuity, or first annual payment for the land.

Harrison said he did not make policy, the president of the United States did. He explained that President

Prophet, a Shawnee religious leader, led an attack on Harrison that began the Battle of Tippecanoe.

Thomas Jefferson, and now President James Madison, thought it best that the Indians settle down on farms like white men. He argued that the Native Americans had more land than they could use efficiently. Anyway, most would rather have money than excess land. Otherwise, they would not sell it.

The Shawnee chief shouted at the interpreter: "Tell him he lies," or words to that effect.[3] The scene got ugly. Tecumseh's warriors rose with knives in hand. Harrison drew his sword. Mrs. Harrison herded the children indoors, where armed soldiers were hiding. The chief and the governor stared one another down. The council fire was put out.

Tecumseh later sent an apology to Harrison for losing his temper. The two met again the next day. Witnesses recorded what the proud chief said. He had a message for President Madison.

> I hope the Great Spirit will put sense enough into his head to induce him to direct you to give up this land . . . he is so far off, he will not be injured by the war. He may sit still in his town and drink his wine, while you and I will have to fight it out."[4]

With that threat, the warriors left Vincennes.

Word got around that the Prophet and the Shawnee tribe had put a price of two thousand beaver skins on Harrison's head. This meant they would pay someone a large sum to kill Harrison. Judge Symmes wrote his son-in-law about the rumor. He joked: "Tell him if he will pay that much for mine, I will bring it to him."[5]

Harrison took the threat to white settlements seriously. He wrote to President Madison and to Kentucky Governor Charles Scott. He requested troops be sent at once to Indiana. Tecumseh was also recruiting allies from tribes near and far. He went as far as Alabama, trying to persuade warriors there to join his Indian confederation.

President Madison sent the Fourth Regiment, an army of regular soldiers from New England. It was led by Colonel John P. Boyd of Massachusetts. Harrison called up the state militias of Indiana and Kentucky. They arrived in Vincennes in late summer. Harrison was the senior officer, and Colonel Boyd served under him. At this time, the regulars, who were professional soldiers, and the militia, who were part-time citizen-soldiers, were often disrespectful of one another. The regulars thought the militiamen were undisciplined amateurs.

The combined forces marched two hundred forty miles north from Vincennes to Prophetstown. It was near the Tippecanoe River in what is now the city of Lafayette, Indiana. Harrison arranged a meeting with Indian leaders for the next day.

Tecumseh had ordered his brother not to start any fights while he was gone. But the Prophet urged an attack on Harrison's sleeping army. He told the Indians that his magic spells would turn the Americans' bullets to water.

The trusting warriors invaded the camp before dawn.

Campfires had been left burning. When the soldiers awoke and jumped up, the firelight outlined their bodies against the dark sky. They made easy targets for the Indians. Harrison reacted immediately and courageously. He personally led the counterattack. The two and one-half hour battle was fierce and bloody. To their surprise, the Native Americans fell wounded and dying. The Prophet's magic did not protect them from the swords and guns of Harrison's men.

When the Indians retreated, Harrison ordered his men to burn Prophetstown. The angry Indians turned on the Prophet. He was fortunate to escape alive. Tecumseh returned to find his village destroyed. His army had disbanded. His foolish brother had ruined his careful plan. Harrison had great respect for Tecumseh's ability. The Indian spies the Americans employed would have told the

The Battle of Tippecanoe lasted two and a half hours. Both sides lost many men, but General Harrison and his forces triumphed over the Native Americans led by the Prophet.

governor that Tecumseh was away recruiting. It was an opportune time for Harrison to have provoked a battle.

William Henry Harrison's action at what became known as the Battle of Tippecanoe received national attention. The losses were about equal on both sides. But Harrison was able to claim victory. He destroyed Tecumseh's plan of uniting all the tribes in one powerful army.

After Tippecanoe, Harrison fought a difficult battle in

Harrison's victory over the Indians at the Battle of Tippecanoe in the Indiana Territory earned him both acclaim and criticism.

the newspapers. Some news reports criticized Harrison. They blamed him for allowing campfires after dark. Some even criticized him for risking his own safety by visibly leading the charge.

To most Americans, especially in the states bordering the Ohio River, Harrison was a hero. But Colonel Boyd, the commander of the Fourth Regiment, complained to Congress and the War Department. He told them the militia was useless. He blamed Harrison for refusing to discipline them. This was the beginning of the rumor that Harrison was too good-natured to be an effective military commander. It was true that he tried to motivate men rather than punish them.

After Tippecanoe, there was a brief peace on the frontier. Tecumseh's dream of an Indian confederation ended with this demoralizing defeat. But it did not stop his intention to rid the Northwest of the white settlers. For military support he now turned to the British in Canada.

Governor Harrison knew a war with England and its Indian allies was coming. Grouseland was no longer a safe place for young children. In the summer of 1812, Anna and the children left their Indiana home. They went to Cincinnati, where they lived in a rented house downtown, awaiting word from the frontier.

WAR OF 1812

Governor Harrison's war with Tecumseh in the Indiana Territory turned out to be a warm-up act for the War of 1812.

Americans disagreed about the need for war with Great Britain. During a prolonged war between France and Great Britain, American ships were the primary neutral carriers of cargo between the United States, the West Indies, and Europe. Great Britain violated the neutral rights policy and boarded American ships. Sailors, who were British deserters and even naturalized citizens, were impressed, or kidnapped, and forced back into the brutal British Navy. Most Americans were outraged in 1807 when a U.S. Navy ship, the *Chesapeake*, was fired upon. War seemed likely then, but President Jefferson fought back with an embargo rather than war. Under the Embargo Act of 1807, no exports were allowed out of the

United States and no imports were allowed in. By 1812, the New England states, whose economy depended upon trade with England, were defying the embargo. They were opposed to war. But war fever was strong in the new western states. People said they were fighting for national honor. But some brash leaders admitted war was an opportunity to take over Canada from the British. And many Westerners welcomed war as an excuse to drive England's Indian allies from the frontier.

Harrison's victory at Tippecanoe encouraged the "war hawks" in Congress. Many of them were from the West. Henry Clay of Kentucky became Speaker of the House of Representatives. Sentiment for war was especially strong in his state. Kentuckians wanted war to end what they called the "Indian problem." Clay bullied the reluctant president, James Madison, into supporting military action. Congress declared war against England in June 1812.

The United States was physically and psychologically unprepared for war. The nation had only a small professional army. President Jefferson had cut government spending to a minimum. There were few military supplies, and only a handful of ships. The federal treasury was almost empty. The people of the New England states threatened to boycott the effort. Governor Harrison must have known it would not be an easy fight. Still, he let the president and Congress know he would like to be named a general.

However, the bad newspaper articles about Tippecanoe had hurt Harrison's reputation. President Madison ignored his offer. Instead, he called up several aged Revolutionary War generals. Governor of the Michigan Territory, General William Hull, was made commander in the West. When the British and Indian armies arrived at Detroit, Michigan, Hull surrendered without a fight.

Another Revolutionary War figure, General James Winchester of Tennessee, was appointed to succeed Hull. He was no better. The Western Army had to be recruited primarily from the Kentucky militia. They would not join Winchester. The Westerners were through being polite. Governor Isaac Shelby told President Madison that his Kentuckians idolized Harrison and would fight for no one else. Harrison had to be in charge. Finally, in September 1812, Madison made Harrison commander-in-chief of the Army of the Northwest. Harrison's interest was now with the military. Late in 1812, he resigned as governor of the Indiana Territory.

Former President Thomas Jefferson was now advising President James Madison on war strategy. He wrote him that conquering Canada was a "matter of marching."[1] James Monroe, the secretary of war, ordered Harrison to immediately recapture Detroit and invade Canada. But this was a task easier said than done.

There was no ammunition left in the West. General Hull had lost it all at Detroit. General Harrison's first task was to find food and equipment to supply the Army. In 1812, feeding an army was difficult and expensive. The main beverage and medicine was whiskey. There was usually plenty of it. Food consisted of flour for bread and beef cattle. The animals had to be driven along the forest paths. They left the roadways to graze, and many times dinner ran away.

Cincinnati was the point of departure for the campaign. The armies had to travel the length of Ohio. From Cincinnati to Lake Erie was more than two hundred miles.

The great Black Swamp began forty miles south of Lake Erie. In summer and fall, knee-deep water covered a vast area. The heads of men and beasts were wrapped in cloth to keep off the enormous mosquitoes. Supply wagons were impossible to move through the muck.

The Kentucky militia had arrived at Cincinnati in summer clothes. They expected a brief campaign. But there were many delays. It was cold in late fall when Harrison's army finally camped near Lake Erie. He begged the women of the West to make warm clothes for the militia. They responded to his plea by sewing thousands of heavy shirts by hand.

The War Department was pushing General Harrison for action. He planned a winter march on Detroit when the swampland would be frozen and passable.

General James Winchester had stayed on to fight under Harrison. He was commanding a division near present-day Toledo, Ohio. Settlers in nearby Frenchtown, Michigan, begged the soldiers to drive out a few British troops that were annoying them. Without waiting for Harrison's approval, Winchester marched to Frenchtown, which was located along the River Raisin. After months of near starvation, the soldiers were enjoying good food and comfort. Then a large army of Canadians and Indians marched into town while the Americans slept. The Kentucky militia put up a good fight, but they were outnumbered. General Winchester surrendered. The British promised his men would be treated properly as prisoners of war.

Winchester, looking foolish in his nightclothes, and the other officers were taken into custody by the British officers. The soldiers who were wounded too badly to travel were left unprotected. British guards looked the other way while their Indian allies tortured and murdered the prisoners. It was a heart-breaking massacre, and "Remember the River Raisin" became the battle cry of the Western Army.

Harrison's Canadian invasion plans were put on hold. He decided to winter at the Maumee River rapids and built a fort at what is now Perrysburg, Ohio. It was named Fort Meigs for the Ohio governor, Return Jonathan Meigs. The stockade was high on a bluff of the river. It covered ten acres. Tents for the entire army could be pitched in the enclosure. Blockhouses for riflemen anchored each corner. Inside the enclosure, the men dug trenches and threw up giant earth mounds, called traverses. When they hid behind the mounds, they would be protected from enemy fire. When construction was finished, Harrison drilled his men for hours. He knew an attack would come.

Harrison did not have to wait long. A siege began at Fort Meigs in April 1813. Tecumseh's Indian army came quietly by land. The British came proudly up the Maumee River in a formation of sailing ships. They brought big guns, which they mounted on a hill across the river. The cannons were aimed at the fort. But the fort was exceptionally strong. British cannon balls did little damage to the thick logs of the stockade. The walls were high. The Indians became discouraged when they could not scale the walls and break into the fort. Tecumseh sent word inside, challenging Harrison to come out for one-on-one combat. The general wisely declined.

Eventually, the Indians realized there would be no prisoners to scalp or rob. Many drifted away. In May, with supplies running short, the British sailed away. Harrison had survived the siege with relatively few losses. Spring

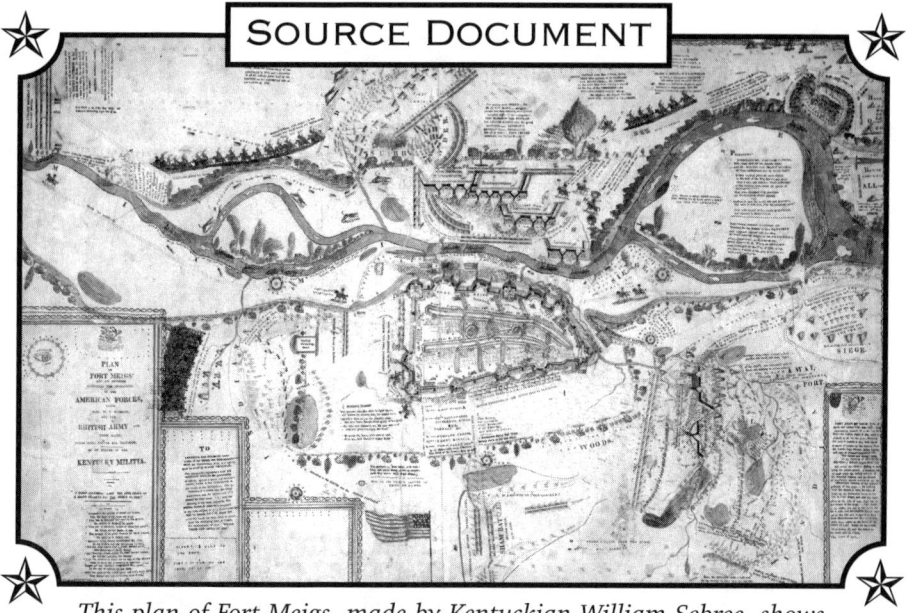

This plan of Fort Meigs, made by Kentuckian William Sebree, shows the sieges of the fort that took place in the spring and summer of 1813.

rains had turned the tent city into a sea of mud. Food was scarce and many soldiers were ill. Yet Harrison and his army had prevailed. This was the first American land victory of the War of 1812. The weary nation was elated.

From the beginning, Harrison said that the United States could not invade Canada unless it controlled Lake Erie, which would allow them to bypass the British stronghold of Detroit. Harrison told the War Department it needed a navy there. Secretary of War John Armstrong finally moved to put a navy on Lake Erie. Commodore Oliver Hazard Perry, a brilliant young naval officer, was sent to Presque Isle (now Erie, Pennsylvania). His mission was to build ships, then take control of the lake.

Perry's small fleet was ready in August 1813. But he had too few sailors to operate the ships. When he asked

This intricately carved powder horn, made by Francis Tansel at Fort Meigs in 1813, features a map of the fortification.

Harrison for help, the cavalry (soldiers mounted on horses) rushed to the lakefront. The men fenced a grassy point near the harbor. Here, their horses were put to pasture. The soldiers then became sailors aboard Perry's ships.

At this time, the British Navy was the strongest in the world. But Oliver Perry defeated the British fleet at the Battle of Lake Erie in September of 1813 at Put-in Bay. It was one of the most famous battles of the war. Commodore Perry scribbled a message to General Harrison on an old envelope. His words of victory have come down in history. The note read, "We have met the enemy, and they are ours."[2] Harrison was overjoyed. Perry's victory gave the Americans control of Lake Erie.

The main body of Harrison's Army sailed to Canada with Perry. The general sent Colonel Richard Johnson with his mounted Kentucky militia by land. Harrison's combined forces were close to three thousand. He was expecting nearly that number from the British. But many of the

Oliver Hazard Perry's forces defeated the British Navy at the Battle of Lake Erie in September 1813. Perry's victory granted control of Lake Erie to the Americans and helped win the war.

The Battle of the Thames, in which Tecumseh was killed, was another victory for General Harrison and the American Army. Tecumseh had worked to unite American Indian tribes against the U.S. troops in order to protect their land.

Canadian militia had left when their terms expired. Weary of the long campaign, many of Tecumseh's Indian followers had left as well. The British supply line was cut when the Americans took control of Lake Erie. Short of food and ammunition, the British Army was forced to retreat.

The Americans easily captured Fort Malden at Detroit. British General Henry Proctor had fled. Tecumseh and some of the Indians went with him. Harrison decided to go after them. At the village of Chatham on the River Thames, Tecumseh finally persuaded Proctor to stand and fight. It was the Indians' last chance to save their homeland. Harrison had high regard for Tecumseh. The Indian was an able, courageous leader. He was also an honorable man. Neither allowed mistreatment of prisoners of war.

At that time on the western frontier, atrocities—scalping and mutilation of prisoners and the dead—were common to both sides. Harrison and Tecumseh were worthy opponents. Both men played by the rules.

Harrison and Tecumseh met for the last time at the Battle of the Thames. The brief battle took place on October 5, 1813. The American Army overwhelmed its opponents. The British fired only three volleys. The Indians fought bravely until the noble Tecumseh was killed— some thought by Colonel Johnson, who was never certain. Proctor and thirty fellow officers were captured. The Americans seized $1 million worth of supplies. It was a decisive victory for General Harrison. The war in the Northwest was over.

8

CIVILIAN LIFE AND ELECTED OFFICE

News spread of Commodore Oliver Perry's victory on Lake Erie. Then America heard of General William Henry Harrison's victories in Canada. The nation went wild. The war in the West was won.

People talked excitedly of making Harrison commander of the Army of the East, which was battling British Canadians near Niagara Falls. After the Battle of the Thames, Harrison and Perry sailed east across Lake Erie. They arrived at Buffalo, on the U.S. side of the falls, on October 25, 1813.

There, Harrison received a letter from Secretary of War John Armstrong. There was no mention of a promotion or new command. Instead, Armstrong gave the victorious general liberty to visit his family. In military code, Harrison read this as an invitation to quit. He had spent fourteen grueling months in the field. This was a poor reward.

General Harrison stopped at the major eastern cities on his way home. He was honored at lavish banquets in New York City, Philadelphia, and Washington, D.C. He was being mentioned as a future political candidate. But Harrison was disappointed not to receive a new command. Oliver Perry was shocked. He expected his comrade would be appointed commander-in-chief for the entire Army. Instead, the secretary of war had undercut Harrison's authority. Armstrong even questioned Harrison's honesty. Tired of John Armstrong's insults, Harrison resigned his commission as general in 1813. This was well before the war ended in 1815. Armstrong made Andrew Jackson a general in Harrison's place.

Armstrong proved to be an incompetent commander. He allowed the British to invade Washington and torch the White House in 1814. The president and the federal government had to leave town in a hurry. It was a national disgrace, and Armstrong was forced to resign.

Madison sent word to his peace commissioners in Europe to end the war as quickly as possible. They accepted peace terms that left things as they were before the war. Not aware the war was over, General Andrew Jackson fought and won the Battle of New Orleans. Although it was meaningless, Americans thought the war ended with a victory. Jackson became the new national hero.

Many lives had been lost in the War of 1812, and the expenses were high. Wartime activities had some positive economic effects, though. Government spending for the military spurred growth in the Old Northwest Territory. Farmers prospered as their crops brought high prices.

Before the war, American industry had not yet taken off. Most manufactured products sold in the United States came from England. But during the war, most foreign trade was stopped. Americans had to buy homemade products. As a result, industries sprang up in the United States. The new industries provided many jobs. The war also solved some of America's transportation problems. Marching armies cut roads through the wilderness. Good roads were important to the young nation. They united the different sections of the country. Farmers and manufacturers were able to move their products to distant markets. Prices rose for farm products, and a land boom began.

Cincinnati was an exciting place to be in 1814. After the Battle of the Thames, settlers flocked to the area. Most came by way of the Ohio River. They stopped at Cincinnati for supplies before moving further west. Cincinnati was the fastest-growing city in the nation. It was the "Queen City of the West," America's original boomtown.

When Harrison arrived home from the war, he found his friends were busily borrowing money for speculation in land. Some were starting factories and other businesses. There seemed to be opportunities to build a great city. Business owners also hoped to make money. Harrison became a partner in an iron works that employed one hundred fifty men. He opened a distillery, where grain was made into whiskey. He became a stockholder in the Miami Exporting Company, which collected goods for river transport to the New Orleans market. The firm was also a bank. It was easy for him to borrow money there.

Family responsibilities also demanded General Harrison's attention at this time. His father-in-law was dying. John Cleves Symmes had once enjoyed immense wealth and position in the Northwest Territory. But Symmes had sold some land before it was surveyed, and he had sold some sections twice. The house and barns of Judge Symmes' expensive estate at North Bend had been destroyed by an arsonist. All of his papers and land records were lost. There were copies of some records at the county court because landowners with bad titles had filed law suits against him. Harrison spent years trying to settle the estate.

Judge Symmes left more debts than cash, but the Harrisons inherited thousands of acres of his land. In 1814, the family expanded the North Bend log house into a spacious frame house and moved from Cincinnati to

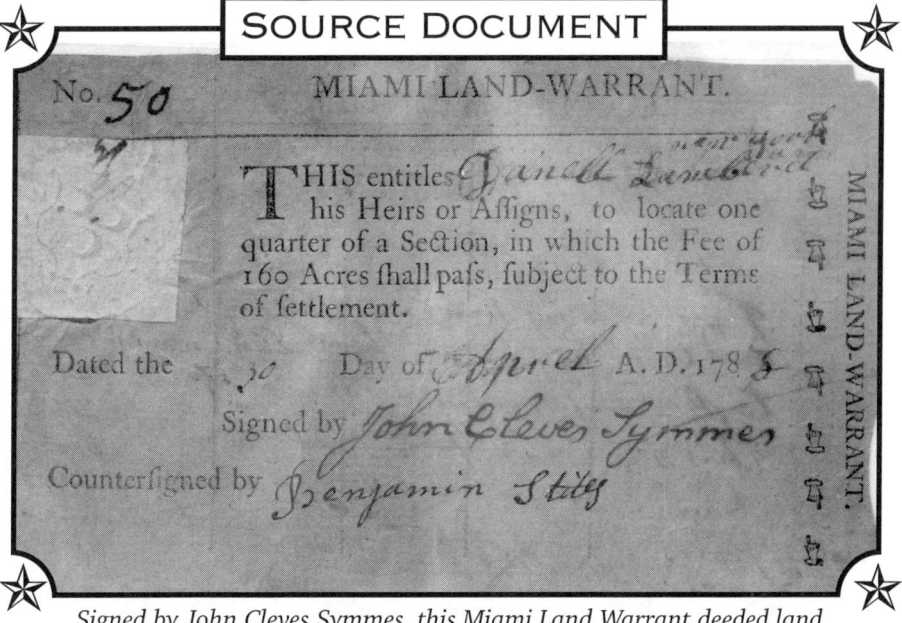

SOURCE DOCUMENT

MIAMI LAND-WARRANT.

No. 50

THIS entitles _____, his Heirs or Assigns, to locate one quarter of a Section, in which the Fee of 160 Acres shall pass, subject to the Terms of settlement.

Dated the ___ Day of _____ A.D. 178_

Signed by *John Cleves Symmes*

Countersigned by *Benjamin Stites*

Signed by John Cleves Symmes, this Miami Land Warrant deeded land to a buyer. After Symmes's death, Harrison had to settle his father-in-law's estate and deal with title issues on properties he had sold.

North Bend. The new house had a large dining room, numerous bedrooms, and a garden gazebo office for Harrison. A tutor was hired to come to the big house to give school lessons to the younger Harrison children. The yard was planted with formal gardens that went downhill to the river. It was an impressive place. Steamboat captains blew their whistles in salute as they went by.

The former general had plenty to do. President Madison asked him to work with the Indians on treaties. Some Ohio tribes had fought on the side of the Americans in the War of 1812. Harrison wanted to see that his promises of land for them were kept. But it was not a pleasant job. Many white people in the old Northwest disliked all Indians. They wanted them eliminated. Many Indians felt the same way about the whites.

Harrison was also being urged by friends to run for Congress. At that time, military service was often the road to a political career. Newspapers reported the Indian wars and the battles of the War of 1812 in detail. Winning generals became popular heroes; losers were subject to ridicule. Americans discussed military and political battles as often as they talk about professional sports today.

General Harrison was a hero in his hometown. He was easily elected to Congress as a Democratic-Republican in 1816. This time, Harrison traveled alone to the capital in Washington, D.C. Anna and the children stayed on the farm in North Bend.

Harrison's Kentucky neighbor, Henry Clay, was the powerful speaker of the U.S. House of Representatives. He appointed the general to committees dealing with the military. Harrison obtained pension payments for widows and orphans of men killed in the War of 1812. Along

Henry Clay's political goals of improved transportation and infrastructure to help farmers and businesspeople were know as the "American System." As a congressman, Harrison adopted many of Clay's ideas.

with Clay, he criticized General Andrew Jackson for his conduct in the Seminole Indian War in Florida, where Jackson had illegally executed a British prisoner. Jackson never forgave the two congressmen.

The Federalist Party lost power when it opposed the War of 1812. Practically everyone was a Republican. But some of the Federalist ideas were adopted by Henry Clay's Republicans. Clay wanted a strong central government. He thought the government should pay for internal improvements such as roads and canals. These improvements would help farmers and business owners market their products. Transportation improvements would lower prices, allowing city dwellers to buy cheaper goods. Harrison agreed with Henry Clay's ideas, which were known as "American System" ideas.

In Congress Harrison fought against a bill that would have taken away the right to buy land on credit. He spoke against cash-only sales. Congressman Harrison said the plan would "foster the interests of the rich," as it would "grind the poor and keep them in a state of vassalage."[2] (Vassals were peasants in Europe who worked the land for lords without hope of ever being landowners.) Early

SOURCE DOCUMENT

H. R. No. 101.

FEBRUARY 27, 1816.

Read twice and committed to a Committee of the whole House on Thursday next.

A Bill

Providing for the sale of the tract of Land, at the British Fort at the Miami of the Lake, at the foot of the Rapids, and for other purposes.

1   *Be it enacted by the Senate and House of Representatives of*
2   *the United States of America, in Congress assembled,* That so
3   much of the tract of land of twelve miles square, at the "Bri-
4   tish Fort of the Miami of the lake, at the foot of the rapids," ceded
5   by the Wyandots, Delawares, Shawanoes, Ottawas, Chippewas,
6   Patawatamies, Miamis, Eel River, Weeas, Kickapoos, Pianka-
7   shaws, and Kaskaskias tribes of Indians, to the United States,
8   by the treaty of Greeneville, of the third of August, one thou-
9   sand seven hundred and ninety-five, shall, under the di-
10   rection of the surveyor general, be laid off into town lots,
11   streets, and avenues, and into out lots, in such manner and
12   of such dimensions, as he may judge proper: *Provided,* the

This document from the United States House of Representatives in 1816 records a motion brought forth by Representative Harrison.

Americans believed the United States should be a place where everyone could become a landowner and a homeowner.

Harrison's own life experiences gave him faith in the nation's progress. He had seen how Cincinnatians had prospered in just twenty-five years. When he arrived in 1791, there had been a few crude log houses on the mud banks of the Ohio River. Now his friends and business partners lived in fine brick mansions with libraries and flower gardens.

For several reasons, Harrison decided not to return to Congress in 1819. Congressional pay was low. Harrison had laid out the town of Cleves near North Bend, and was trying to sell building lots. A depression had begun in the United States in the summer of 1818. It hit hardest in the West, where farm prices fell and banks foreclosed on homes and farms.

Money was scarce, and Harrison wanted to focus on making his large farms profitable. He read books and magazines about farming. He exchanged letters with other gentlemen farmers. They were looking at the best breeds of animals and the best seeds for growing crops. Harrison wanted to help other local farmers improve the quality of their livestock and crops. In 1819, he organized an agricultural society in the Cincinnati area. Today it is known as the Hamilton County Agricultural Society. Harrison was the society's first president. He started a county fair, which quickly became a regional attraction. Henry Clay came from Lexington, Kentucky, to attend one of the fairs with Harrison. Farmers brought their farm produce to the event. Prizes were awarded for the best things on display. The fairs became a popular form of entertainment. Today the Hamilton County Fair is still a popular annual event.

Cincinnati's pioneer families thought they had the time and money to improve education and culture. In 1819, Harrison's friend Judge Jacob Burnet started the Cincinnati College. Congressman Harrison was a donor and member of the first board of trustees. Dr. Daniel Drake, another friend of Harrison's, led the drive to establish the first Episcopal Church in Cincinnati. Harrison, already a supporter of the Presbyterian Church, became a donor and a vestryman at Christ Church Episcopal.

In 1816, Congress granted a charter to the second Bank of the United States. This was a privately owned corporation that was given the exclusive right to handle federal tax money. Judge Burnet and Congressman Harrison accepted appointments to the board of a branch of the bank when it opened in Cincinnati. At first, businesses welcomed the bank. They thought it could loan them money to build even more factories and stores.

Many ambitious and optimistic people borrowed money from the bank. Everyone who could borrow a few hundred dollars was speculating in land. It became addictive, almost a form of gambling. The buyers did not intend to build upon the land, or to farm it. They intended to keep it only until the demand and the price went up. Then they expected to sell it at a big profit. No one thought the price would go down. And speculators thought there would always be people willing and able to buy their land. By the summer of 1819, however, the prosperity boom had started to go bust.

In 1819 Harrison ran for the Ohio State Senate. It met less frequently than Congress and would take up less of his time. In the campaign, he was criticized for his ties to the banks. However, he was elected and went to Ohio's capital in Columbus.

In the Ohio legislature, politicians were excited about building canals that would connect the rivers to Lake Erie. The inland waterways would help farmers get their crops and livestock to market. Harrison served on two committees that worked to build canals in Ohio. He took real interest in these projects. He knew the geography of Ohio from his travels with the military, and he gave good advice.

As an Ohio state senator, Harrison dealt with a money issue related to the banks. In 1820, the Cincinnati branch of the Bank of the United States told borrowers they must repay their loans immediately. This is known as "calling a loan." The bank demanded people repay in "hard" money—gold or silver, not paper money. There was not much hard cash available in the West, and those who could not pay lost their property. Harrison managed to sell some farm acreage to pay his debts, which were rumored to be as much as thirty thousand dollars. His best friends lost their fine houses.

The city building boom stopped. Skilled workmen and laborers lost their jobs. Few people had cash; they traded goods or work for food. The bank was depicted in cartoons as a many-headed monster that gobbled up people, businesses, and smaller banks. People blamed the monster bank for their losses. And they blamed the bank's directors, including Harrison.

Harrison endured a string of bad luck in the years that followed. He lost a three-way race for governor in 1820. In 1821, Harrison lost a bid for the U.S. Senate. He lost an election for Congress in 1822. Most observers blamed his connection to the bank for his string of losses. Others said his 1819 vote in Congress to allow slavery in the Arkansas Territory had offended abolitionists (those who opposed slavery). But Harrison's district had very few antislavery voters. And only a few brave politicians spoke out for abolition. The most likely reason for Harrison's rejection by voters is that then, as now, people voted with their pocketbooks. When the economy is bad, and pocketbooks are empty, voters punish the most likely suspect.

The 1820s were uncertain times for most politicians. The Democratic-Republican Party was splitting. It broke into two parties: the Democratic Party, led by General Andrew Jackson, and the new National Republican Party, led by Henry Clay. Harrison went with Clay. The National Republicans, who would soon take the name of Whigs, were the party of the American System. Party members were united chiefly by their belief in a strong federal government, tariffs (taxes on imports) to protect native industries, and tax support for transportation systems.

Just when it looked like Harrison's political career was over, the tide turned. Harrison was a presidential elector for Henry Clay, who ran for president in 1824. This meant Harrison's name was on the ballot. As part of the electoral college, the body of voters who elect the president, voters knew he was pledged to cast his electoral vote for Clay. Clay lost the national race, but Harrison carried Ohio for him. And he helped the new National Republican Party elect a majority in the Ohio legislature.

9

SENATOR AND U.S. MINISTER

The Ohio legislature with its National Republican majority elected William Henry Harrison to the U.S. Senate in 1825. (Direct election of senators by the people did not begin until 1913.) This was Harrison's most important office so far. President John Quincy Adams was in the White House at this time. The bitter presidential race of 1824 had ended with Adams' selection by the House of Representatives over General Andrew Jackson.

Life in Washington was interesting, but work was demanding. Harrison talked of his busy schedule in a letter to his wife. "I am obliged to devote a part of the morning to exercise—without which I would not be able to live here," he wrote.[1]

For exercise, the senator went horseback riding before breakfast. Washington was then a cluster of government buildings in the country, and cross-country riding was popular. In the military, Harrison had learned the value of physical fitness for performance. He stayed slim and fit all his life.

There were many meetings to attend and letters to write. Like other senators, Harrison proposed laws in papers called bills. A bill might be a request for new funds. It could be a new right—like pensions for war widows or free education for war orphans. If other members of the House of Representatives and the Senate voted to approve a bill, it became law when the president signed it.

Senator Harrison was chairman of the Committee on Military Affairs and the Committee on the Militia. He wanted to provide free and universal military training in the schools. He thought that in a nation relying on citizen-soldiers, all young men should be prepared. This bill did not pass. But Harrison was successful in passing bills that provided funds for the U.S. Military Academy at West Point, Army chaplains, and veterans' pensions.

Harrison was a practical politician, but he was idealistic about some things. He was a patriot and loved his country. He believed the Union of the United States must be preserved at all costs. He had great faith in democracy —government run by the people.

Harrison and his friends in Washington, D.C. watched the revolutions being fought in South and Central America during the 1820s. Harrison's friend Henry Clay was secretary of state at this time. Clay wanted the United States to help the patriots who were struggling for independence from Spain in Mexico and Colombia. He suggested sending representatives to these countries.

Clay knew Harrison shared his love of democracy, and he persuaded President John Quincy Adams to make

SENATOR AND U.S. MINISTER

This drawing of William Henry Harrison was made around the time of his appointment as U.S. minister to Colombia.

Harrison the first U.S. minister to Colombia. General Simón Bolívar had led the revolution there against Spain. Now he was at war with neighboring Peru.

Harrison had never left the country except to chase British troops into Canada in the War of 1812. But he accepted the appointment to South America. The position was a great honor. It also carried a handsome salary—nine thousand dollars a year. There was another nine thousand for expenses. Harrison found the additional income welcome. He had a large property to maintain. There were children at home to feed, clothe, and educate. He had sent his sons to expensive colleges—Transylvania in Lexington, Kentucky, and Miami University in Oxford, Ohio—and to professional schools for law or medicine.

Even the grown sons sometimes turned to Harrison for financial help. Symmes Harrison was the federal land registrar in Vincennes and lived at Grouseland, which the family still owned. He had made a bad loan of five thousand dollars and lost his job. His father had to help Symmes and his family. Another son, William Henry Harrison Jr., was a talented lawyer in Cincinnati. But he liked gambling and drinking more than working. He became an alcoholic and quit practicing law. As a result, Senator Harrison had another family to support.

Harrison resigned his Senate seat and left for Colombia on November 11, 1828. He sailed from New York aboard the *Erie*, a U.S. warship. By that time, there were signs that General Andrew Jackson would defeat President Adams in the fall elections. Apparently, Harrison did not worry about losing his new job under a new president. American presidents generally kept most officeholders. And Harrison had a talent for making friends across party lines. He had been appointed governor of the Indiana Territory by three presidents of differing political parties. He very likely thought his luck would hold. Otherwise, he would not have made such a long and expensive journey by sea, wagon, and horseback. The trip to South America took more than two months.

Anna Harrison remained in North Bend. Seventeen-year old Carter, the youngest son, went along as his father's secretary. Harrison rented a fine home in Bogotá, the capital of Colombia. He shipped furniture and china there for entertaining. He took seeds from his farm and planted a large garden. Native hostesses were delighted when he brought vegetables—celery, turnips, and radishes—and salad greens to their dinner parties. In Colombia, Harrison found exotic plants and birds to admire. A number of specimens went home with him. For many years, a colorful macaw lived in the front yard trees at North Bend. It startled visitors with its squawking.

As predicted, General Jackson, a Democrat, defeated President John Quincy Adams, who ran as a National Republican. Jackson, the self-styled "people's president," was inaugurated on March 4, 1829. Four days later, he fired Harrison and appointed a Kentuckian as minister to Colombia. Even Democrats were shocked at Jackson's

SENATOR AND U.S. MINISTER

One of Jackson's first acts as president was to revoke Harrison's appointment as minister to Colombia. He then refused to send a ship to bring the general back from South America.

discourteous treatment of a fellow war hero. Harrison had been in Bogotá a little more than one month.

Jackson and Harrison were almost complete opposites in personality and in politics. Jackson was born in poverty, but he became wealthy. His Tennessee estate, the Hermitage, was a large property worked by many slaves. Jackson distrusted businessmen and big government. He opposed tariffs that helped manufacturers and hurt Southern planters. He even disapproved of government support for canals and roads. Jackson hated big banks, especially the Bank of the United States.

Jackson had been a stern military commander. He practiced flogging, dueling, and speedy execution of deserters. As president, he ruled like a general. He refused to cooperate with Congress. He ignored decisions of the Supreme Court. But Harrison and Jackson agreed on the need to preserve the Union. They were both fierce nationalists and patriots.

Minister Harrison was insulted at being removed from his Colombian post. But he was not sorry to leave Bogotá. He was disappointed with the government of Colombia. General Simón Bolívar had been expected to liberate the people to enjoy self-government, but Harrison did not see that happening. Instead, he saw a military dictatorship continuing after the revolution. In the United States, citizen-soldiers returned to farm and factory when the war was over. In Colombia, they wanted to be soldiers for life. It appeared that Bolivar would become a king rather than an elected president. Harrison strongly disapproved. He believed in the American way. When he left Colombia, Harrison wrote a long letter to Bolivar. He expressed his hope that Colombia would soon become a democracy like the United States. He later published the document.

The government ship that was supposed to meet Harrison's party did not show up. While he waited, the former minister met a traveling businessman, Silas Burrows, at the seaport of Carthagena. Burrows, who had been a young soldier in the War of 1812, sent Harrison's group to New York on his private yacht. The gentleman asked for nothing in return. But Harrison had a way of remembering favors. Years later, when he was in the White House, Mr. Burrows was one of his few dinner guests.

10

Clod-Hopper Candidate

William Henry Harrison's ship arrived in New York City in February 1830. Friends held dinners there in his honor. And they plotted revenge against Democratic President Andrew Jackson. Back in Cincinnati, there was a welcome banquet held in Harrison's honor at Madame Trollope's Bazaar, an exotic new building on the site of old Fort Washington.

The 1830s did not begin happily. The Harrison family suffered a great personal loss. Their oldest son, Symmes, died suddenly. He had been married to Clarissa Pike, the daughter of the famous explorer Zebulon Pike. The family had returned recently from Indiana, and had no income or property, so the widow and grandchildren moved in with Anna and William Henry at North Bend.

For Cincinnati, 1832 was the "Year of Disasters." A great fire destroyed the business district. Then the Ohio

River flooded the valley. At Harrison's farm in North Bend, the fields were filled with debris from the flood. Farm animals and fences were swept away. That summer there was no rain and crops failed. Cholera, a deadly disease, swept the nation. It reached Ohio in September, and lasted for thirteen months. More than eight hundred Cincinnati residents died. Business and social life almost stopped in the city. Country people like the Harrisons stayed on the farm.

Despite the disasters, people kept migrating West. The population of Cincinnati grew 260 percent, to 24,831 people, between 1820 and 1830.[1] New people arrived, bringing new ideas. Anna and William Henry became friends with Professor Calvin Stowe and his wife, Harriet Beecher Stowe. A Presbyterian minister, Calvin Stowe came to Cincinnati in 1832 to teach at Lane Seminary.

On August 20, 1833, the Stowes were overnight guests at North Bend. At the time, the Harrison family was giving land to build a Presbyterian church near their home. Late that night a Harrison grandson was born in the house. The parents were Elizabeth and John Scott Harrison. The baby, Benjamin Harrison, would one day become the twenty-third president of the United States.

Harriet Beecher Stowe was a fiction writer. Her stories appeared in local and national newspapers. After she left Cincinnati, Mrs. Stowe wrote a famous antislavery novel called *Uncle Tom's Cabin*. It was based upon her Ohio experience. The Ohio River was the dividing line between the free North and the slave South. An organization known as the "Underground Railroad" was active along the river, helping slaves escape.

As a student, William Henry Harrison had been a

member of a humane society in Richmond, Virginia. Its members discussed the problems connected with slavery. As an adult politician, Harrison said he hated slavery. But he consistently disapproved of abolitionists, who wanted to set slaves free immediately by an act of Congress. Harrison believed the federal government could free the slaves only by purchasing them from their owners. He expressed his views at Cheviot, Ohio, in a July 4, 1833 speech. He said then that he "looked forward to the day when the North American sun would not look down on a single slave."[2] Later, in his presidential campaigns, when asked for his position on a number of topics, Harrison referred people to this speech.

General Harrison was one of the most popular personalities in Southern Ohio. He got lots of requests to give free speeches, usually on patriotic subjects. But he had no steady income. A farmer's earnings are always dependent on the weather and market prices. By 1834 the Harrison family was in serious financial trouble. Harrison still had friends in local politics. In 1834, the judges of Hamilton County appointed him clerk of courts. This seemed like a lowly position for a former U.S. senator and ambassador, but it paid very well, as much as ten thousand a year, depending on the amount collected from court fees. Harrison's son Carter was in Cincinnati studying law, and he helped his father run the office. Most folks concluded the old general could no longer win an election. People felt sorry for him. They thought his political career was over.

Harrison was sixty-two years old in 1835 when his friends began to talk him up as a presidential candidate. There was a new political party that had grown out of the

Harrison's daring military exploits made him an attractive candidate for the Whig Party. This political ribbon commemorated Harrison as the "Hero of Tippecanoe, Fort Meigs, and Thames."

CLOD-HOPPER CANDIDATE

Martin Van Buren did not come from a wealthy background, but the Whig Party managed to present him as well-to-do and out of touch with the common people. In contrast to "King Matty," as Van Buren was known, Harrison was promoted as a friend of the common man.

National Republican Party. It was called the Whig Party. Seeing how popular Andrew Jackson was, Whig leaders were looking for a comparable military hero to run for president. They were also looking for a candidate from the West, where so many voters had gone. General Harrison came to mind. Cincinnati newspapers promoted Harrison. Then eastern papers picked up the message. Harrison was not shy. He told party leaders that if they wanted this "Clod-hopper," the lowly clerk of Hamilton County for president, he was available.[3] (Clod-hopper is a term for a poor dirt farmer.) The child of Virginia aristocrats was presenting himself as an ordinary man of the frontier.

President Jackson refused to run for a third term in 1836. He insisted that Martin Van Buren be the Democratic nominee. The Baltimore convention approved Van Buren without discussing another candidate. Whigs screamed that "King Andrew" had named a crown prince, and that the country was headed toward hereditary monarchy.

Martin Van Buren was a smart New York state politician. He had managed Jackson's winning campaigns and built a national political organization for the Democrats.

"Harrison, Our Country's Hope," read this ribbon, which was distributed to the many "Tippecanoe Clubs" throughout the country.

The party had team members in every part of the country. These people could be counted on to organize other people in what was called a "grassroots" operation. Long before the Internet, telephone, or even the telegraph, the team members contacted voters, and one another, by writing letters and knocking on doors.

The Whigs were a young, unorganized political party. They could not agree on one candidate to support. Nicholas Biddle, the former president of the Bank of the United States, came up with the Whig campaign strategy. Instead of one man, he decided the Whigs would run three. General Harrison represented the West. Daniel Webster of Massachusetts was supposed to carry the North. Hugh Lawson White of Tennessee was expected to win in the South. No candidate would win a majority, and the election would be decided by the House of Representatives, which the Whigs controlled. That was Biddle's plan.

Harrison approached this political campaign the way he would a military campaign. Critics said he was too old and worn down to run. To disprove this, he worked tirelessly, traveling the country. He began with the nearby states of Indiana, Kentucky, and Illinois. Everywhere he went, huge crowds gathered. In Indiana, he attracted a large and enthusiastic crowd at a reunion of Tippecanoe battle veterans.

Next, he toured the great eastern cities of Washington, Baltimore, New York, and Philadelphia. People flocked to see him. Some came out of curiosity. They knew his name from history lessons or from their war veteran fathers. But they stayed to cheer his speeches. They loved this old hero who looked like a plain, friendly farmer.

Biddle's plan backfired when the three Whig candidates divided the vote, letting Van Buren win by a large majority. But Harrison ran a strong second. He carried eleven states. His friends saw they had a chance to elect a western man next time. The Harrison campaign did not end in 1836. It just kept going to prepare for 1840.

Log Cabin to the White House

Despite his good showing in the election of 1836, William Henry Harrison was not guaranteed the Whig nomination for president in 1840. Three months into Martin Van Buren's term, the Financial Panic of 1837 began. It developed into a serious economic depression. Many people were out of work. Most were short of cash. President Van Buren and the Democrats said the economy was not the responsibility of government. But people blamed him for their misery, and they were angry that he did not seem to care.

A Whig candidate seemed certain to win the next presidential election. Henry Clay, who actually built the Whig Party, figured that he could finally win in 1840. Whig leader Thurlow Reed did not care who their candidate was or what he believed. He cared only about putting a Whig in the White House. Party leaders would support the candidate most likely to win.

The Whigs held their first national convention at Harrisburg, Pennsylvania, in 1839. There were twenty-six states then. Nearly every state sent representatives to the convention. The delegate from far-away Arkansas arrived after the vote was taken, so he cast his state's vote for the nominee.

Senator Henry Clay of Kentucky was the early favorite. But delegates from several of the larger states did not believe he had popular support. He was well known, but not all of his fame was positive. He was a slave owner, and northern antislavery voters found that unacceptable. Reed and his big money backers liked Clay, but they were afraid he would lose. To the bankers and businessmen, losing was unacceptable. General Winfield Scott was, for a time, the favorite of the northern delegations. But he had made a strong antislavery statement, which made him unacceptable to the South. At last, the convention decided upon General William Henry Harrison. He was a moderate, middle-of-the-road politician. And he was a well-known war hero who could appeal to East, West, North, and South.

John Tyler, a former Democrat who had joined the Whigs because he disliked Jackson's policies, was the Whig's vice-presidential nominee. Tyler's family owned a plantation on the James River in Virginian, not far from the Harrison birthplace. The Whig Party hoped to attract southern Democrats with Tyler on the ticket.

Democratic newspapers immediately attacked William Henry Harrison. Some writers called him "granny." They said he was failing in mind and body. Harrison's military record was the subject of lengthy discussion. He was accused of being overly cautious and even cowardly. Some suggested he had botched the battle at Tippecanoe, and that Richard Johnson (who became vice president of the United States under Martin Van Buren), was the true hero of the Battle of the Thames.

General Harrison took to the road to show he could outrun his younger opponent. The physical energy and fighting spirit that Harrison displayed as a young soldier stayed with him almost to the end of his life. At a time when travel was mainly by horse-drawn coach, canal boat, and river steamboat, the elderly candidate maintained an amazing schedule.

Harrison gave his first big campaign speech at Columbus, Ohio, in June 1840. From there, he traveled north by horse-drawn coach. He took what was only the second railroad ride of his life, beginning about fifty miles south of Lake Erie. At the lake, he boarded the steamer *Perry,* named for his old military friend Oliver Perry. The steamer took him to Maumee Bay, and into Fort Meigs. Here, on June 11, the Log Cabin campaign held a mass meeting that made national news. People were drawn to the rallies out of curiosity. Everyone wanted to know, as the campaign song asked: "What has caused this great commotion, motion, motion/Our country through?"[1]

The spirit of the gatherings was similar to a religious camp revival meeting. Such outdoor meetings had begun around 1820 in Kentucky. They became especially popular in the South and the West. Like the Log Cabin campaign meetings, revivals featured group singing, long sermons, and picnic fare.

The Whigs held rallies across the nation, even when

LOG CABIN TO THE WHITE HOUSE

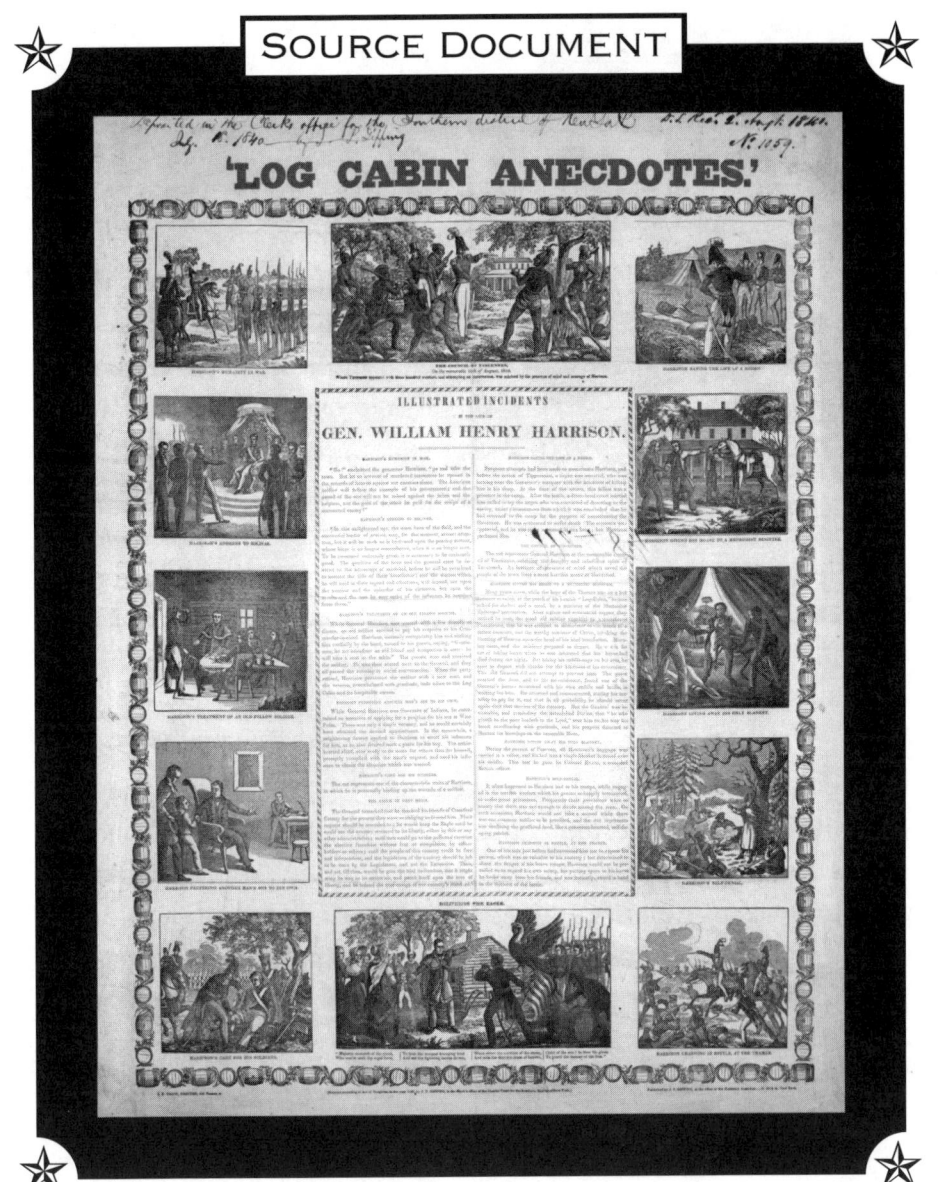

SOURCE DOCUMENT

This engraving features twelve scenes from the life of General Harrison. Bordered with cider barrels, it was printed in 1840 to build support for the Whig presidential ticket.

83

Harrison's 1840 running mate, John Tyler of Virginia.

General Harrison could not be present to speak. The campaign committee had money to spend. Large contributions came from bankers and businessmen in the eastern United States and even Great Britain. The committee hired excellent stump speakers to travel from town to town. Some became popular entertainers, like John Baer, a country blacksmith with a gift for comedy. Others, like Tom Corwin of Ohio and Abe Lincoln of Illinois, were ambitious young politicians who volunteered to campaign for Harrison.

The Harrison campaign rallies drew wildly enthusiastic supporters. Inspirational speakers reminded people they lived in a great country that was unlike any other in the world. The message was patriotism and faith in the promise of American life. People were worried about not having enough money, and the Log Cabin campaign meetings made them feel better. There, people laughed and sang and cheered for Harrison and Tyler, whom they hailed as "Old Tippecanoe and Tyler Too."

1840 was a year of personal sorrow as well as triumph. Harrison was in Springfield, Ohio, in mid-June, when word came that his son, Dr. Benjamin Harrison, had died. This was the third of his sons to die in three years. William Henry Jr. had died in February 1838 and Carter had died in August 1839. The Springfield speech was

This log cabin in Hartford, Connecticut, was erected on July 4, 1840, by supporters of William Henry Harrison's Log Cabin campaign. Tippecanoe Clubs sprang up around the country to support Harrison.

cancelled. The general returned to North Bend to console Mrs. Harrison and the many grandchildren who filled the big house. He had only one son left to help with the farm, and a major construction project was under way. The Whitewater Canal was being built through a corner of his property. Harrison was supplying wood and stone from his farm.

Even when he stayed home for a few days, political allies and strangers appeared—most times uninvited—at his country home. The candidate welcomed them as he did family and old friends. They were invited in for conversation and a good meal. In one year, the household consumed three hundred sixty-four hams, plus other roast meats, platters of home grown vegetables, and pastries. Harrison and his wife Anna entertained generously even when they were sad and struggling to make ends meet.

Grassroots campaigning was and still is necessary to a successful political campaign. General Harrison, who was sixty-seven years-old, did not make as many long-distance trips in 1840 as he did in 1836. But except for the month following Benjamin's death, he was highly visible in the West. Fortunately, the Whig Party organization had a stable of speakers, glee clubs, and representatives who canvassed every state.

The Whig Party also financed campaign newspapers. The most successful, *The Log Cabin,* was run by Horace Greeley. Whig papers wrote glowing stories about General Harrison the war hero, and about Farmer Harrison, who lived in a log cabin with a coonskin nailed to the wall. Newspaper cartoons pictured the Whig candidate as a kindly old farmer welcoming an injured war veteran with a handshake and a glass of cider. In contrast, they depicted Harrison's Democrat opponent, President Martin Van Buren, as a city slicker in fancy dress.

President Martin Van Buren was not born to a wealthy family. But he made money as a successful lawyer. He was a capable administrator who was president at a difficult time. The depression, which hit America shortly after he took office, was worldwide. Money issues are always difficult for politicians to explain and for most people to understand. But Van Buren also had an image problem. He liked fine clothes and fancy carriages. He dressed in rich velvet suits and wore French kidskin gloves. People accused him of putting on airs more suited to a king than the president of a democracy. Newspaper articles gossiped that "Prince Matty" wore girdles and perfume. Cartoons pictured him primping before mirrors. His manners became a national joke.

Van Buren also liked rich surroundings. He ordered White House decorations that were frightfully expensive. For example, he spent $1,307.50 for three window curtains. Whigs in Congress learned about the bill for this and other fancy furnishings ordered by the president. They read the long list on the floor of Congress. It was published in all the newspapers. People were shocked and angry. They were doing without necessities, and the president was stocking up on luxury items.

The Democrats did not defend President Van Buren against unfair attacks on his character. Instead, they talked about the bank or the subtreasury plan. The independent treasury, with subtreasuries in different states, was a simple idea that Van Buren had developed. It placed government money in independent government banks, eliminating the need for dealing with private banks. But people were tired of hearing about such complicated things. Young Whigs interrupted Democrat political meetings by bursting into songs from the Log Cabin song books. How could anyone talk about issues when a group was chanting, "Van, Van is a used up man"?[2]

It was obvious by mid-summer that Harrison, the Farmer of North Bend, would win. And he did. The election results showed the electoral vote was 234 to 60 for Harrison. The Whigs won 19 of the 25 states. "Tippecanoe and Tyler Too" lost their home state of Virginia. But the ticket won New York, Van Buren's home state.

The remarkable thing about this election was the number of voters, which increased by 60 percent from 1836. For the first time, each candidate polled over 1 million votes. William Henry Harrison had 1,274,624; Martin Van Buren 1,127,781. About 900,000 more voters appeared at the polls than in 1836.[3] The states were gradually eliminating tax and property ownership restrictions for voters. That was one reason for the big increase. But more important was the enthusiasm that came with the Log Cabin campaign.

The good news of Harrison's election reached Cincinnati about a week after the results were announced in Washington, D.C. Celebrations started immediately. President-elect Harrison resigned his position as clerk of courts. Letters and visits from office-seekers began at once. Harrison had kept an open door all his life. But now there was not a moment of peace. The weary old gentleman had difficulty turning people away.

"I wish," said Mrs. Harrison, "my husband's friends had left him where he is, happy and contented in retirement."[4]

In January 1841, the president-elect received an affectionate send-off from Cincinnati. Mrs. Harrison was too ill to accompany him. John Scott Harrison, the only remaining son, stayed behind to run the farm. A widowed daughter-in-law, Jane Irwin Harrison, went along to be the White House hostess. The trip to Washington by steamboat and horse-drawn coach was long and tiring. But Harrison was cheered by the throngs of well-wishers along the way.

President-elect Harrison arrived in the capital on February 9, 1841, his sixty-eighth birthday. He called upon President Van Buren, who greeted him with kindness and courtesy. The president hosted a dinner at the White House for his successor and the leaders of both political parties. Van Buren found Harrison to be a "most extraordinary man," who did not seem to be impressed with the importance of his new role. But Van Buren noted that Harrison was "as tickled with the Presidency as is a young woman with a new bonnet."[5]

Harrison visited Congress and former President John Quincy Adams. He made a quick tour of the capital. Then, Harrison retreated to his childhood home in Virginia to prepare for the inaugural and the months ahead. But his proud family did not let him rest. The days and evenings were filled with gatherings of relatives and neighbors.

Harrison wrote his inaugural address at Berkeley Plantation while sitting at a desk in the same room where he had been born. Sometimes he referred to the histories of Greece and Rome that he had read as a schoolboy. President-elect Harrison was willing to run for office as a "clod-hopper" farmer, but he wanted this speech to demonstrate his classical education to the world.

Daniel Webster, the brilliant senator who was to become Harrison's secretary of state, helped edit the speech. And while Webster boasted that he had killed off many Roman senior statesmen with his pencil, the speech was still too long. It was the longest presidential address ever given.

The March 4, 1841 Inaugural Day was cold and damp. Tippecanoe clubs marched with log cabin floats and live raccoons in cages. Military bands played. President Harrison, who was proud of his equestrian skills, rode his spirited horse, "Old Whitey," in the procession.

The inaugural parade halted at the east porch of the Capitol. The president wore no overcoat or hat. He stood for nearly two hours in the open air, reading his patriotic address. The population of the city of Washington was forty thousand then. An estimated fifty thousand people were in the audience.

The president talked at length about the Constitution and the balance of powers it had established. He promised to live up to the ideals of the founders. He would not initiate laws, and never veto one made by Congress, unless it appeared to him clearly unconstitutional. What he meant was, he would not be an imperial president like the Whigs thought Andrew Jackson had been.

President Harrison went to work quickly. He met every day with his cabinet. A special session of Congress was scheduled for March 31. The Whigs had promised to take politics out of government work. Harrison issued an executive order to officeholders. They were forbidden to participate in politics or to make campaign contributions.

President Harrison was surprised to find the White House had no Bible. He bought one at a local bookstore. He went to church twice each Sunday, attending the Episcopal Church in the morning and the Presbyterian Church in the evening. In Cincinnati, he had long been a member of both congregations.

Washington society was amused to see the president out early at the public markets. Harrison had enjoyed the

William Henry Harrison's March 4, 1841 inauguration.

farmers' markets in Cincinnati and Colombia. He bought food for the White House cooks to prepare. He gave a number of fine dinner parties. But he missed Anna and home-style food. On March 26, the president wrote to his son, John Scott Harrison. He asked him to bring Mrs. Harrison to Washington. And he inquired when the shipment of beef and bacon would arrive from North Bend.

Several weeks after the inaugural, the president was drenched in a rain storm as he returned from the market. He developed a cold. On March 27 he admitted he was not well and sent for a physician. Bed rest was prescribed. When the president's condition did not improve, medical treatment became more intense. A variety of remedies were tried—doctors bled his veins, blistered his skin with hot suction cups, and gave him stimulants such as brandy, and sedatives such as opium.

The patient did not respond. Instead, with the ill-advised "help" of his doctors, he grew worse. The cabinet and his friends and family watched over him. But the

President Harrison's deathbed.

White House did not tell the people or the press that his condition was serious. On April 4, 1840, Harrison addressed those at his bedside: "I wish you to understand the true principles of the government. I wish them carried out. I ask nothing more."[6] Then he passed away, apparently from pneumonia.

Harrison was the oldest man elected to the presidency until Ronald Reagan. And he was the first president to die in office. He had lived a healthy and strenuous life, without serious illnesses. It is possible he might have recovered had he not received medical treatment. In August 1841, the *Boston Medical and Surgical Journal* published an article criticizing the methods used to treat him.[7]

Mourning ribbons, like this one, were distributed following Harrison's death in 1841.

The nation was shocked by the unexpected death of President Harrison. Mourning was sincere and deep. So many people had seen and cheered "Old Tip." He had inspired the love and admiration of the masses. The outpouring of grief was greater than any displayed since the death of George Washington. John Johnston, a federal government Indian agent in Ohio, reported the sadness of the Indians who had high expectations of their friend in the White House. "Their confidence in his justice and humanity was unbounded," Johnston wrote.[8]

Mrs. Harrison was packing to leave North Bend for the White House when word came of the death of her husband. First Lady Anna Harrison never made it to the White House. But she was the first presidential widow to receive a congressional settlement—one year's salary of twenty-five thousand dollars. She continued to live in the family home at North Bend until it was destroyed by fire in 1858. She died in 1864, at the age of eighty-nine.

John Scott Harrison led a delegation from Cincinnati to bring his father's remains home. The casket was transported by a special black-draped train to a river steamer, the *Raritan*. The voyage back home reversed the route of Harrison's trip East as president-elect. Crowds gathered along the railroad tracks and the river banks as the casket of "Old Tip" passed by. In February, the huge crowds had greeted their hero with shouting, singing, and gun salutes. In July, the onlookers were silent and tearful.

Ohio's first president was entombed at a hillside spot in North Bend. It was a gravesite he had selected, overlooking the Ohio River. Today, a tall limestone obelisk pierces the western sky. It stands atop a wooded knoll at the base of Mount Nebo. The monument rises six stories over Harrison's tomb. It is carved with the record of his legendary career:

> Ensign of the 1st United States Infantry
> Commandant of Fort Washington
> Hero of Tippecanoe
> Major general of the War of 1812
> Victor of the Battle of the Thames
> Avenger of the Massacre of the River Raisin
> Secretary of the Northwest Territory
> Delegate of the Northwest Territory to Congress
> Territorial governor of Indiana
> Member of Congress from Ohio
> Ohio state senator
> United States senator from Ohio
> Minister to Colombia
> Ninth president of the United States

Harrison's tomb overlooks the river from what was once the heart of his three thousand acre estate. North Bend is still a small, beautiful, and somewhat remote village. And William Henry Harrison remains its most distinguished resident.

12

Legacy

Former President John Quincy Adams was outraged that John Tyler should become president with the death of William Henry Harrison. He described Tyler as "a political sectarian of the slave-driving, Virginian, Jeffersonian school, principled against all improvement."[1]

The Whig Party never recovered from the loss of President Harrison. As president, John Tyler ruined the hopes of party leaders. Some years later, newspaper publisher and reformer Horace Greeley reflected upon the impact President Harrison's death had upon the party and the country. He wrote that America had lost abler men, but "none she could so ill spare since Washington."[2]

Henry Clay had hoped to restore the Bank of the United States and put through all the programs Andrew Jackson and Martin Van Buren had vetoed. John Quincy

Adams expected to finally realize his dream to establish the Smithsonian Institution. When Tyler vetoed a number of bills on public works, disgusted Whig leaders turned him out of the party.

The Whigs elected only one more president—General Zachary Taylor in 1848. He died after one year in office. The party, which was united primarily by being anti-Jackson, lost support at the local level. Many of the Log Cabin Whigs, including its brightest light, Abraham Lincoln, moved on to form the new Republican Party.

The Harrison campaigns of 1836 and 1840 set the style for future presidential campaigns. But the national campaigns that followed did not attract the same spontaneous enthusiasm. It was hard to duplicate the appealing theme of the Log Cabin campaign. There, the songs, the souvenirs, and the friendly farmer of North Bend came together most winningly.

After 1840, as the nation moved toward the Civil War, politics became more sober. The frivolity of the Log Cabin campaign may have seemed inappropriate. But the emphasis on grassroots campaigning endured for more than one hundred years. The practice of door-to-door, person-to-person contact by the candidate or representatives continued until recent times. When television came into popular use, tactics changed. Electronic media messages beamed into private homes made personal contact less important. Today, presidential candidates use television and the Internet to reach the most voters.

William Henry Harrison was the last president to be born before the American Revolution. He was the first to die in office, and he served the shortest term. He left a political legacy in his family. His son John Scott Harrison was a two-term congressman from Ohio. John Scott's son, Benjamin Harrison, became the second President Harrison. He was part of the only presidential grandfather-grandson combination when he was elected in 1888. Tippecanoe Clubs were reactivated then by men who had voted for William Henry Harrison. Benjamin saved the letters with Tippecanoe campaign ribbons that he received from these old voters. Today, they are in the Library of Congress.[3]

William Henry Harrison did not live long enough to leave a legacy as president. But his activities in the years before 1841 helped define the young nation. As much as any American leader, he shaped the character of the Old Northwest.

As aide-de-camp to General Anthony Wayne in 1795, Harrison played a lead role in the Battle of Fallen Timbers. The battle, along with the Treaty of Greenville, opened the Northwest Territory to settlement. As the first territorial delegate to Congress, Harrison authored the Land Act of 1800, which brought countless small farmers to the West. He was the first and only governor of the Indiana Territory, which at one time included Upper Louisiana.

William Henry Harrison was the representative western leader. He tried his hand at all the opportunities the raw frontier offered. He served the public as Army officer, civil servant, and elected representative. And he was equally enterprising as a private citizen. He was a devoted gardener and farmer, landowner, town planner, banker, industrialist, and philanthropist.

Harrison's enthusiasm for civic and business ventures was contagious. With visionary citizens such as Judge

President Harrison, who became ill shortly after his inaugural and died of pneumonia a month later, was the first U.S. president to die in office.

Jacob Burnet, General James Findlay, and Dr. Daniel Drake, Harrison helped make Cincinnati in 1840 the fastest-growing city in the nation.

Harrison's legacy is most visible in Ohio and Indiana. There, he worked to bring religion, education, and culture to cities and farms in the wilderness. His leadership and gifts built churches, elementary schools, colleges, libraries, and agricultural societies. Vincennes University in Indiana and the Hamilton County Agricultural Society in Ohio are among those that have survived to this day.

William Henry Harrison led by his example and deeds. He was always an officer and a gentleman. He faced the dangers and uncertainties of life in the wilderness with rare courage and a spirit of accommodation. He treated his fellow men—rich and poor, red, black, and white, servant and nobleman—with the habitual courtesy and kindness that were a part of his nature. He was an effective military commander, but he was not a violent man.

We can judge William Henry Harrison only by what he was, not by what he might have been as president. His love for the Union, his fellow soldiers, and his adopted West drove his public life. He achievements are reflected in the title he earned before he was elected president.

"Who is General Harrison?" Congressman Robert Johnson, a Democrat, asked on the floor of the House of Representatives in 1830. "He is the son of one of the signers . . . the history of the West is his history."[4] And so it was.

President Harrison was proud to be identified with the development of a peaceful, prosperous, and civil society in the West. No republic in the ancient world was as blessed or as promising as Cincinnati when Harrison left it for the national capital in 1841.

President William Henry Harrison had the satisfaction in his lifetime of being known as the undisputed "Father of the West."

Chronology

1773—William Henry Harrison born February 9 at Berkeley Plantation in Virginia.

1787—Attended Hampden-Sydney College.

1791—Studied medicine in Philadelphia; father died; Harrison joined military as ensign, was sent to Fort Washington.

1794—Aide to General Anthony Wayne in successful Battle of Fallen Timbers; promoted to captain by Wayne.

1795—Signed Treaty of Greenville which opened the frontier; served as Commandant of Fort Washington; married Anna Symmes at North Bend.

1796—Daughter Betsey Bassett born at Fort Washington.

1798—Appointed secretary of the territory of the U.S. Northwest of the River Ohio by President Adams; a son, John Cleves Symmes, born at Fort Washington.

1797—Bought land and log cabin in North Bend, Ohio.

1799—Elected territorial delegate to Congress; introduced the Harrison Land Law of 1800.

1800—Appointed governor of the Indiana Territory; a daughter, Lucy Singleton, born in Richmond.

1801—Harrison and family moved to Vincennes, capital of the Indiana Territory.

1802—A son, William Henry II, born in Vincennes.

1803—Reappointed governor of Indiana and made governor of Upper Louisiana; began construction of Grouseland.

1804—A son, John Scott, born in Vincennes.

1806—A son, Benjamin, born in Vincennes.

1809—Negotiated with Indians for 3 million acres in Treaty of Fort Wayne; Daughter Mary Symmes, born in Vincennes.

CHRONOLOGY

1810—Confronted by Tecumseh and Indian Confederation at Vincennes.

1811—Defeated Prophet at Tippecanoe River; son Carter Bassett born in Vincennes.

1812—Appointed major general and commander-in-chief of the Army of the Northwest by President James Madison.

1813—Siege of Fort Meigs; Detroit recaptured; Harrison defeated British and Indian forces; a daughter, Anna Tuthill, born in Cincinnati.

1814—Resigned from military; inherited 3,000 acres and moved to North Bend, Ohio.

1816—Elected to 14th and 15th Congress; attended sessions in Washington, D.C.

1817—Last child, James Findlay, born.

1819—Founded Agriculture Society in Hamilton County; elected to Ohio Senate.

1820—Lost bid for Ohio governor; planned first county fair for Agricultural Society.

1821—Lost contest for U.S. Senate; Harrison's Cincinnati bank and foundry business failed.

1822—Lost campaign for U.S. Congress.

1825—Elected to U.S. Senate by the Ohio legislature.

1828—Appointed minister to Colombia by President John Quincy Adams

1829—Removed from Colombia post by Andrew Jackson.

1833—Defined national political views in Cheviot, Ohio, July 4th speech.

1834—Appointed Hamilton County Clerk of Courts.

1836—Ran for president on the Whig ticket.

1840—Holds Log Cabin campaign and wins the presidential election, with 19 of 25 states.

1841—Inaugurated March 4; died in White House on April 4; buried at North Bend.

Did You Know?

Events from the President's Lifetime

Did you know that in 1803 the United States bought the Louisiana Territory from France for $15 million? This purchase was made at the urging of President Jefferson and included 800,000 square miles from the Mississippi River to the Rocky Mountains, making up the present day states of Louisiana, Arkansas, Oklahoma, Missouri, Kansas, Nebraska, Iowa, South Dakota, Wyoming, Minnesota, Colorado, North Dakota, and Montana.

Did you know that the British Army burned the White House in 1814 while at war with the United States? During the conflict known as the War of 1812, the British battled Americans on United States soil, invading Washington, D.C. Dolley Madison, wife of President James Madison, was forced to flee the White House as the British Army advanced, but she refused to leave until a famous portrait of George Washington had been taken down from the wall and carried to safety.

Did you know that the Erie Canal opened in 1825, spanning 363 miles to connect Albany and Buffalo, New York? This canal created a waterway between the eastern and midwestern states, opening up new markets and creating a population boom in the upper Midwest. New York City Harbor became the most important waterway in the world as a result of the Erie Canal.

Did you know that a slave revolt led by Nat Turner killed more than fifty whites in 1831? Turner was a slave in Southampton, Virginia, who believed he had been called by God to lead his people out of slavery. He organized a group of slaves and launched an insurrection that resulted in the killing of his master's family and other local white people. Though seventy-five slaves joined Turner in the rebellion, they were soon defeated and Turner was later captured and executed.

Chapter Notes

Chapter 1. The Log Cabin Campaign
1. Robert Gray Gunderson, *The Log-Cabin Campaign.* (Louisville: University of Kentucky Press, 1957), p. 117.

Chapter 2. A Child of the Revolution
1. Clifford Dowdey, *The Great Plantation: A Profile of Berkeley Hundred and Plantation Virginia from Jamestown to Appomattox* (Charles City, Virginia: Berkeley Plantation, 1957), p. 296.

2. Mark Thorburn, *Berkeley Plantation's Most Famous Resident: William Henry Harrison, The Hero of Tippecanoe,* (Point Roberts, Washington: Mark Thorburn, 2000), p. 5.

Chapter 3. An Officer and a Gentleman
1. James A. Green, *William Henry Harrison: His Life and Times* (Richmond, Virginia: Garrett and Massie, Incorporated, 1947), p. 25.

Chapter 4. Aide to Anthony Wayne
1. A.E. Jones, *Early Days of Cincinnati, Columbia and North Bend* (Cincinnati, Ohio: Cohen & Co., 1888), p. 130.

2. Freeman Cleaves, *Old Tippecanoe: William Henry Harrison and His Time.* (Originally published 1939 by Charles Scribner's Sons) (Newton, Connecticut: American Political Biography Press reprint, 1990), p. 21.

Chapter 5. Family Man and Governor
1. Freeman Cleaves, *Old Tippecanoe: William Henry Harrison and His Time.* (Originally published 1939 by Charles Scribner's Sons) (Newton, Connecticut: American Political Biography Press reprint, 1990), p. 23.

2. James A. Green, *William Henry Harrison: His Life and Times* (Richmond, Virginia: Garrett and Massie, Incorporated, 1947), p. 61.

3. Beverley W. Bond, Jr., *The Intimate Letters of John Cleves Symmes and His Family* (Cincinnati: Historical and Philosophical Society of Ohio, 1956), p. 98.

4. Bond, p. 98.

5. Green, p. 65.

6. Rowland H. Rerick, *State Centennial History of Ohio* (Madison, Wisconsin: Northwestern Historical Association, 1902), p. 153.

7. Green, p. 350.

8. Daniel K. Richter, *Facing East From Indian Country: A Native History of Early America* (Cambridge, Massachusetts: Harvard University Press, 2001), p. 227.

Chapter 6. Battle of Tippecanoe
1. James Hall, *A Memoir of the Public Services of William Henry Harrison of Ohio* (Philadelphia, 1836), p. 114.
2. Hall, p. 115.
3. Hall, p.116.
4. Hall, p.119.
5. James A. Green, *William Henry Harrison: His Life and Times* (Richmond, Virginia: Garrett and Massie, Incorporated, 1947), p. 120.

Chapter 7. War of 1812
1. Richard N. Current et al. *American History: A Survey* (New York: Alfred A. Knopf, 1975), p. 285.
2. Freeman Cleaves, *Old Tippecanoe: William Henry Harrison and His Time.* (Originally published 1939 by Charles Scribner's Sons) (Newton, Connecticut: American Political Biography Press reprint, 1990), p. 187.

Chapter 8. Civilian Life and Elected Office
1. Jacob Burnet, *Notes on the Early Settlement of the North-Western Territory* (Cincinnati: Derby, Bradley & Co., Publishers, 1847), p. 393.
2. James A. Green, *William Henry Harrison: His Life and Times* (Richmond, Virginia: Garrett and Massie, Incorporated, 1947), p. 237.

Chapter 9. National and International Service
1. James A. Green, *William Henry Harrison: His Life and Times* (Richmond, Virginia: Garrett and Massie, Incorporated, 1947), p. 257.

Chapter 10. Clod-Hopper Candidate
1. Henry A. and Kate B. Ford, *Cincinnati, Ohio* (Cleveland, Ohio: L.A. Williams & Co., Publishers, 1881), p. 81.
2. James A. Green, *William Henry Harrison: His Life and Times* (Richmond, Virginia: Garrett and Massie, Incorporated, 1947), p. 290.
3. Freeman Cleaves, *Old Tippecanoe: William Henry Harrison and His Time.* (Originally published 1939 by Charles Scribner's Sons) (Newton, Connecticut: American Political Biography Press reprint, 1990), p. 293.

Chapter 11. Log Cabin to the White House
1. James A. Green, *William Henry Harrison: His Life and Times* (Richmond, Virginia: Garrett and Massie, Inc. 1947), p. 355.
2. Green, p. 356.
3. Richard N. Current et al, *American History: A Survey* (New York: Alfred A. Knopf, 1975), p. 898.
4. Freeman Cleaves, *Old Tippecanoe: William Henry Harrison and His Time.* (Originally published 1939 by Charles Scribner's Sons) (Newton, Connecticut: American Political Biography Press reprint, 1990), p. 328.
5. Cleaves, p. 334.

6. Cleaves, p. 342.
7. Green, p. 400.
8. Cleaves, p.342.

Chapter 12. Legacy

1. Lynn Hudson Parsons, *John Quincy Adams* (Madison, Wisconsin: Madison House, 1998), p. 247.

2. James A. Green, *William Henry Harrison: His Life and Times* (Richmond, Virginia: Garrett and Massie, Incorporated, 1947), p. 404.

3. Green, p. 373.

4. Freeman Cleaves, *Old Tippecanoe: William Henry Harrison and His Time.* (Originally published 1939 by Charles Scribner's Sons) (Newton, Connecticut: American Political Biography Press reprint, 1990), p. 279.

5. Cleaves, p.334.

Illustration Credits: Harrison Symmes Memorial Foundation/Photos by Barrett J. Brunsman, 20, 76, 78, 93; Library of Congress, 9, 10, 13, 19, 25, 31, 37, 40, 43, 44, 54, 61, 69, 71, 77, 84, 85, 91, 92, 98; National Museum of Art, Smithsonian Institution, 41; Ohio Historical Society, 7, 52, 53.

Source Document Credits: Harrison Symmes Memorial Foundation/Photos by Barrett J. Brunsman, 22, 59; Library of Congress, 4, 26, 34, 51, 62, 83; National Archives, 16.

Further Reading
William Henry Harrison and his Times

Fitz-Gerald, Christine Maloney. *William Henry Harrison: Ninth President of the United States.* Danbury, Connecticut: Children's Press, 1987.

Gaines, Ann Graham. *William Henry Harrison: Our Ninth President.* Chanhassen, Minnesota: The Child's World, 2001.

Huston, James. *Counterpoint: Tecumseh vs. William Henry Harrison.* Lawrenceville, Virginia: Brunswick Publishing Company, 1987.

Nardo, Don. *The War of 1812.* San Diego: Lucent Books, 2000.

Cwiklik, Robert, *Tecumseh: Shawnee Rebel.* Philadelphia: Chelsea House Publishers, 1993.

Ohio Presidents Series

Painter, Mark P., *William Howard Taft,* Cincinnati: Jarndyce & Jarndyce Press, 2004.

Internet Addresses

Library of Congress
http://www.memory.loc.gov

Ohio Historical Society
http://www.ohiohistory.org

The White House
http://www.whitehouse.gov/history/presidents

American Presidents Life Portraits
http://www.americanpresidents.org

PLACES TO VISIT

Ohio

Cincinnati Historical Society Library and Museum Center, Cincinnati. Researchers come to the library to study the James Albert Green Collection, which contains more then 1,000 titles about William Henry Harrison. Museum exhibits portray life on the western frontier from settlement to the steamboat age. Open year-round. Museum Center: (513) 287-7000, Library (513) 287-7094. <http://www.cincymuseum.com>.

Fort Meigs, Perrysburg. Extensive property owned and operated by the Ohio Historical Society. Excellent reconstructed fort with new exhibits in 2003. Open year-round Wednesday–Saturday 9:30 A.M. to 5 P.M. Sundays noon to 5 P.M. (800) 283-8916. <http://www.ohiohistory.org>.

William Henry Harrison Memorial Tomb, North Bend. The William Henry Harrison Memorial Tomb stands on a knoll overlooking the Ohio River. The tomb contains twenty-four vaults for the bodies of President Harrison, his wife, their son John Scott Harrison, and other members of the Harrison family. The tomb is located in the William Henry Harrison Memorial Park off of U.S. Highway 50 in North Bend, a village in Ohio's Hamilton County.
<http://www.ohiohistory.org>

Indiana

Grouseland, Vincennes. Located at 3 West Scott Street, this elegant Georgian home was built by William Henry Harrison in 1803–1804 while he served as the first governor of the Indiana Territory. It was named Grouseland after the birds Harrison loved to hunt. Grouseland served as a home for Governor Harrison and his family, but it was also a center of government for the Indiana Territory and a fortress for the community in times of trouble. Grouseland is open to the public for tours Sunday through Saturday from 11 A.M. to

4 P.M. in January and February; and Monday through Saturday from 9 A.M to 5 P.M. and Sundays 11 A.M. to 5 P.M. from March through December. Grouseland is closed Thanksgiving, Christmas, and New Year's Day.
(812) 882-2096.
<http://www.grouselandfoundation.org>.

Virginia

Berkeley Plantation, Charles City. Located at 12602 Harris Landing Road, this is the birthplace of William Henry Harrison. The early Georgian mansion sits on a hilltop overlooking the James River. Berkeley Plantation is believed to be the oldest three-story brick house in Virginia and the first with a pediment roof. The original mansion was built in 1726 from bricks fired on the plantation. Berkeley Plantation is open to the public seven days a week from 8 A.M. to 5 P.M.

Book Orders

To purchase copies of this or other books in the Ohio Presidents Series, E-mail quantity price and or P.O. order (library and public entities only) inquiries to booksales@cincybooks.com.

For orders, make check payable to Cincinnati Book Publishing, $14.95 per book, plus $1.05 Ohio tax if applicable, and $4 each S&H. Send total of $20 to:

Cincinnati Book Publishing
2449 Fairview Avenue
Cincinnati, OH 45219
http://www.cincybooks.com

INDEX

A
Adams, John, 8, 31, 37
Adams, John Quincy, 67, 68, 70, 89, 95, 96
Armstrong, John, 51, 56, 57
Arnold, Benedict, 15

B
Bank of the United States, 65, 78, 95
Battle of Fallen Timbers, 27, 28, 97
Battle of New Orleans, 57
Battle of Put-in-Bay, 52
Battle of the Thames, 55, 56, 58, 82
Battle of Tippecanoe, 42–45, 47, 79, 82
Berkeley Plantation, 12, 14, 15, 17, 89
Biddle, Nicholas, 78, 79
Blue Jacket, 27
Bolívar, Simón, 69, 71, 72
Boyd, John P., 42, 45
Burnet, Jacob, 64, 98
Burrows, Silas, 72

C
Chesapeake, 38, 46
Clark, William, 28, 36
Clay, Henry, 47, 60, 61, 63, 66, 68, 80, 81

D
Drake, Dr. Daniel, 64, 98

E
Embargo Act of 1807, 46, 47

F
Financial Panic of 1837, 80
Findlay, James, 98
Fort Greenville, 25, 29
Fort Meigs, 5, 6, 11, 50, 82
Fort Washington, 23, 29, 30, 73

G
Greeley, Horace, 86, 95
Grouseland, 35, 40, 45, 69

H
Hamilton, Alexander, 32
Hamilton County Agricultural Society, 63, 64, 98
Hampden-Sydney College, 17
Harmar, Josiah, 20, 25
Harrison, Anna (Symmes), 10, 29, 30, 32, 35, 41, 45, 60, 70, 73, 74, 85, 86, 88, 91, 93
Harrison, Anne, 14
Harrison, Benjamin (23rd president), 74, 97
Harrison, Benjamin I, 12, 13
Harrison, Benjamin V, 12, 13–15, 32